Lead Generation to Vetting

HOW TO
RESEARCH
FOR TREASURE
HUNTING & METAL
DETECTING

Otto von Helsing

Lead Generation to Vetting—From a veteran researcher

HOW TO
RESEARCH
FOR TREASURE
HUNTING & METAL
DETECTING

Otto von Helsing

ISBN-13: 978-1480186774

ISBN-10: 1480186775

CONTENTS

FOREWORD

There have been many books published on the subject of doing research. This book brings the art of researching into the 21st Century, utilizing 21st Century methods and tools. These methods and tools are explained in a very understandable manner by an author who has been there and done that.

Whether you are seeking leads to follow, researching a local treasure story, doing genealogical research, or any other type of research for business purposes, this book helps to light the way.

Being computer literate is a definite plus in this day and age, and having access to the Internet opens up a wealth of research related information to the person capable of seeking it out. You don't have to be computer literate to utilize much of the information set forth in this book, but if you do have that capability you will find many new sources of information within these pages.

If you are involved in doing research of any kind you need this book, not just on your library shelf, but in your hands, or on your desk. If you are either an amateur researcher or an experienced hand at digging up the information you require, you will find this publication to be of extreme value.

By all means, use the best and latest technology available to you to find what you are looking for, and this book will provide the tools to do exactly that.

J. Karl Foss
Research Unlimited

RESEARCH FLOWCHART

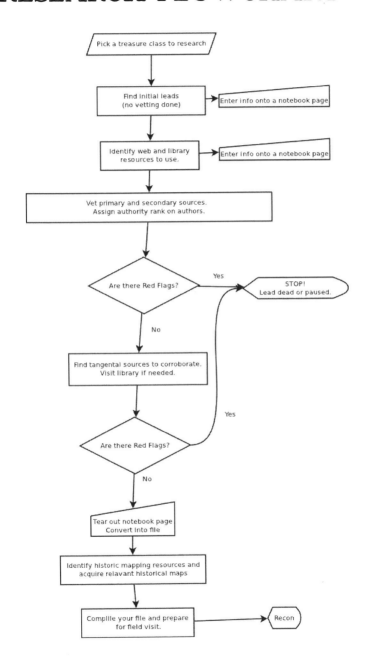

Pick a treasure class to research

Find Initial leads
(no vetting done)

Enter info onto a notebook page

Identify web and library
resources to use.

Enter info onto a notebook page

Vet primary and secondary sources.
Assign authority rank on authors.

Are there Red Flags?

Yes

STOP!
Lead dead or paused.

No

Find tangental sources to corroborate.
Visit library if needed.

Are there Red Flags?

Yes

No

Tear out notebook page
Convert into file

Identify historic mapping resources and
acquire relavant historical maps

Compile your file and prepare
for field visit.

Recon

TREASURE HUNTING RESEARCH

This book is about finding treasure, and finding treasure is all about research.

Yes, research. Pure and simple.

The goal of this book is to teach the average person how to do good research to find promising leads for metal detecting and treasure hunting. I don't care if you have gray hair on your head and hate computers or if you are 20-something and like to text while driving. (In which case, it's likely you won't make it to the gray-hair stage.)

But I'm sneaky; I'm also going to show you how you can research anything. This will be quite handy in your private life or your business, whether you want to background check the guy who's dating your daughter or the technology your company wants to license from a vendor. That is the real value I hope you discover from this book. You spent over $20 on this book. I hope to give you over $1,000 in value if you are willing to learn. The willing-to-learn part is the more important piece of that puzzle.

If you think you don't have to research because you just "get lucky," I've got news for you. You are not special. I don't care what your third grade teacher told you, every successful treasure hunter and detectorist has to do research. It is just part of the game, so let's make this easy for you. I'm going to lay out real research techniques and assets. You just need to absorb and comprehend it.

What you ultimately learn here is not about sources, not about treasure hunting; rather it is all about critical thinking. Once you learn critical thinking skills, you can do research on anything.

ARE YOU READY FOR THIS BOOK?

Probably. If you bought this book or stole it, you are a motivated individual. You are smart enough to realize you need more information on research. This tells me you are ahead of 95 percent of all those who call themselves treasure hunters. So I'd say you are definitely off to a good start.

There are some basic things I'm expecting you to already know about treasure hunting and metal detecting. This isn't an introductory book—it is advanced. You should already know how to use your detector, the Code of Ethics, what treasure is, know to keep your mouth shut, and why you shouldn't eat yellow snow. Just in case you are new to this interesting and sometimes bizarre hobby of treasure hunting, here are some critical books you should read and have in your library:

- Treasure Hunters Manual #6 or #7 by Karl Von Mueller

- The WPA Guide for your state

- Your local county history book(s)

- Your state's Delorme atlas –Of all the commercial atlases, this has the best resolution.

- Treasure Hunter's Atlas by Thomas P. Terry – A negative knock list. If you find a lead which matches one in the atlas, quickly abandon it. The atlas is about legends, and if you throw out any legend as a lead, you will save yourself great amounts of time. Time, you see, is everything.

If you are a casual coinshooter who is tired of clad coins, and if you know you are into the hobby for the fun of being outdoors, this book will help get you to older coins so that you can enjoy your time outside and come home with more interesting coins.

If you are a die-hard serious THer, then sit up, grab a pen, and take notes. I even encourage you to write in the margins of this book as well. This book is jam packed with tools you need.

A FAST AND EASY PROJECT... OR NOT

This theme will recur throughout this book, and hopefully throughout your life if you understand this fundamental truth: Life is short, don't waste it.

I learned one of the great lessons in life from an unexpected place. In college, I had to take a civil engineering course on project management. One of the first lessons they began to drum into us was something called "Planning Fallacy." This is the name for a dangerous fault in human nature—the flaw of overestimating what we can get done and underestimating the time and cost to get it done. I want to pass on this critical lesson in life: You must spend time wisely.

Expect things to take longer than you plan and to spend much more time to get things done than you initially imagined. Don't forget all the hours in support time you have to spend to do proper research and field testing.

- DON'T chase unvetted stories.

- DON'T follow other detectorists to hunted-out grounds.

- DO think for yourself.

- DO believe in your ability to discover great new areas.

- DO research for new areas and DON'T tell where you find good sites. You have many hours invested in finding these sites. Giving away your information means you have to spend many man hours researching and field sampling to find another location."

To drive home the concept, consider this: In 1996, a study was done at a university to get students to predict the length of time they would need to finish a thesis paper. Average predicted (33 days), best case predicted (27 days), and worst case (48 days) estimations were given. In the end, the average actually achieved was 55 days. Ha![1]

So beware the ideas of "This will be a quick project" and "I can get this done fast." It won't be, and you cannot.

There is rarely going to be an opportunity to redo any project you research. So it is important to quickly filter out bad leads and identify resources to vet good-looking leads.

TIME WELL SPENT

For those who want to do things right, the following are my recommendations for several good uses of your time. All of these tools will be addressed later in this book. The time spent with these offers the best bang-for-your-buck return for hours invested in research. Mainly, learn your tools like you would your detector.

1. **Get the Zotero add-on for your web browser** – Spend about one to two hours really learning it. This is a powerful, daily tool you will use for the next 5 to 10 years until a better one comes along that works like it.

2. **Create a Source Deck** – Spend 30 minutes and type out (or copy and paste from your browser) all the good resources you think you already have found. A little explanation on each is good.

3. **Create a free account with Earthexplorer.usgs. gov** – Spend two hours and take the tutorials over at learninggis.com about how to get historical images.

---

1. Journal of Personality and Social Psychology, Vol 67(3), Sep 1994, 366-381.

4. **Explore Archive.org** –Spend one hour browsing the resources. To know Archive.org is to love Archive.org. You can find most of your local county history books here.

5. **Download and learn Freemind or any other mind-mapping tool** – Spend 20 minutes getting the hang of it by outlining one of your upcoming projects, e.g. building a bookcase, installing solar cells, or researching a lead.

CHAPTER ONE

THE PSYCHOLOGY OF RESEARCH

If you dread research, you really bought the wrong book, pal. Nothing I can do for you except wish you the best of luck digging clad coins in the local park.

But if you are on the fence about how much research you should do, I want you to remember that only the winners take home the gold. So hop in, buckle up, and let's get rolling.

HOW TO MOTIVATE YOURSELF TO RESEARCH

I may be an engineer, but I acknowledge that emotions play a role in treasure-hunting research. I've estimated that for every hour I spend in research, I will shave off about 10 field hours of fruitless cache hunting. Remember that your biggest expense is your time. DON'T WASTE IT.

Motto #1: Research brings in more silver. For coin shooters, I've surmised that every four hours of researching will bring in 50 percent more silver per hunt. You're not finding silver now? You will be.

Motto #2: Be motivated by knowing you are avoiding a lot of unnecessary work by researching. I don't have any study I can cite in my defense of either of these two assertions. I have formed them from notes and empirical evidence over two decades.

All OLD coin-producing sites are a depleting resource. They eventually get picked over, and you will have to go back to researching again.

YOU WANT TO BE SWINGING A DETECTOR

We all have that urge to swing a detector and pop up prizes from the good earth, but restrain yourself. Research will take you from swinging that detector over 500 acres to focusing on one good acre.

Motto #3: Research shrinks the target area to find the hot spot. Don't let your detector arm overrule your brain. Work smart, not hard. I expect you to be of a superior breed to the average treasure hunter because you bought this book (or figured out how to steal it), so show it. Slow, steady aim . . . then pull out the detector. Got it?

A DOOMED HUNT

If you don't do research, but you want to find new, fertile ground, then you are just plain screwed. Blind luck isn't a plan, it's just hope. Hope doesn't reward you with good, juicy target ground, time after time after time. Only research can do that.

There is a saying that an expedition's failure is decided long before you ever leave—if you didn't thoroughly research it first. It applies to treasure hunting even more so.

Motto #4: A failed hunt was decided long before you ever left your house. I am not alone in this belief of research first. E. Lee Spence, a noted treasure hunter and marine researcher, considers historical research his "drug of choice." Further he states:

[I] believe the biggest key to success on any expedition is the archival research that precedes it.[2] Do your research, and you will find success.

---

2. Treasures of the Confederate Coast: The 'Real Rhett Butler' & Other Revelations, E. Lee Spence, 1995, p 517, Narwhal press.

CHAPTER TWO

LEAD RESEARCH VS. TARGET EVALUATION RESEARCH

This book covers two types of research. First, you need to just get raw leads. Second, you need to research those leads until you arrive at a go/no-go decision.

Often the two paths—raw leads and research—become intertwined. While researching one lead by finding primary sources, you will inevitably spot interesting stories that hint at lost items, caches left behind, old carnival areas, and other juicy bits of flotsam on the river of history.

> *It is incumbent upon the treasure hunter to learn to recognize a treasure lead when he reads, sees, or hears it.*
> - BOB KATT[3]

---

3. Research for Treasure Hunters by Robert "Bob" Katt, Granville Publications, 1990.

For now, we'll cover obtaining leads; research will be covered in depth later.

CHAPTER THREE

OBTAINING TREASURE LEADS

First, let us clarify the difference between a lead and a project.

A lead is a starting point. A lead becomes a project when the research on the lead looks good and passes the smell test. Leads just start you down a research path. Many will end abruptly when you find negatives that kill the lead. So don't get married to your leads.

What type of lead you seek depends on the class of treasure you seek. You have a desire for leads with the intent to research them. That's good. Now you just need to figure out where you want to go. Every story has a beginning and an end—you simply need to find your beginning.

What do you want to research? Artifacts of ancestors? Old coins? Caches? Old West relics? Moonshiner stuff? Outlaw loot? Drug money? Militaria? Children's lead toys? Mafia victims?

Leads are often just rumor at first. You have to vet them out to develop them into projects. Or a lead could be an oblique reference in a book to something interesting. Are you smart and experienced enough to identify leads when you read one? Can you spot the facts that make a story a lead? Missing money may never be mentioned. It may be a story of the sudden death of a widower or of a farmer and his wife killed in a tornado. Perhaps the local marijuana grower drove his Benz over a cliff. All of these are leads. Your job is to research and find the pluses and minuses to the story.

If you are spanking brand new and want to find your first leads, then obtain and read your local county history book. Not just any history book, your local county one. Look for passages that talk about buildings and take note of where they are—that is a coin-hunting lead. Then look for anyone who was rich and was murdered—that could be a cache lead. Seek out mentions of robberies then research to see if the loot was never found.

Alternatively, you can pull up newspaper archives from the 1950s and seek the same things.

GENEALOGY

There are many treasure leads that will require you to do genealogy. I just thought I'd go in head-first and tell you. This will be a typical research area for cache hunters or those who want to find ancestor stuff.

I'm a rip-off-the-bandaid kind of guy, so you need to know the base truth—learn your genealogy skill well. You will often need the backgrounds of people of interest when vetting a lead.

Knowing how to research genealogy will serve you well and provide you with empathy for that relative who does your family's genealogy. (Every family has someone who goes down the rabbit hole hunting all of the ancestors.)

Further, near the end of your research process, when you are out in the field establishing ground truth and doing reconnaissance, you have a cover story. Just say you are doing research for a local history book or a bit of genealogy. Often, by the end of a deep research stint, you actually could knock out a 50- to 100-page local history book. But more importantly, you will break the social ice and be accepted as an outsider who wants to write about the local area. You may even be invited to seek out the local historian/genealogist who will give you new, tantalizing leads to hunt down.

For a great guide on performing proper genealogy, look up *www.researchguides.net* for their extensive how-to guides. Genealogy involves attacking a problem from so many angles and sources that my book won't even try to tackle that type of research.

Genealogy Research Guides, Tips and Online Records

The Basics of Online Genealogy Research for Beginners and Beyond

Genealogy Research Guides Subject Index	
Birth, Marriage & Death Records	**Birth, Marriage and Death Records - Vital Records**
Cemeteries & Obituaries	• Birth, Marriage and Death Records - Finding Vital Records Research Guide
Census Records	**Cemeteries and Obituaries**
Free Genealogy Stuff	• Cemeteries and Obituaries Research Guides and Online Records
Historical Newspapers	**Census Records**
Military Records	• US Census Records: Research Tips and Clues 1790-1930 with links to online indexes
Naturalization Records	• Some Free Online Census Records and Indexes - USA
Passenger Lists & Records	• State Census Records Guide - Includes Some Online Indexes for censuses taken between or separate from the Federal census
People & Places	• Genealogy Research Guide - Census Records
Genealogy Guides for Beginners	o 1940 Census Records
	o 1950 and Later U.S. Census Records
	Free Genealogy Software, Charts, Forms and Online Records
	• Free Genealogy Stuff - Free Online Records, Databases and Software
	• Free Blank Genealogy Charts and Forms from Ancestry.com includes an ancestral chart (or "pedigree chart" - this is a basic family tree research forms, and more (these charts can be downloaded for free and printed out)
	Military Records
	• Online Military Indexes, Records and Rosters of Soldiers from the Revolutionary War to Vietnam includes the Civil War, World War One and World War Two
	• How to Find World War One Draft Cards 1917-1918
	• Information about Ancestry's World War II Draft Cards Collection
	• Civil War Pension & Service Records - the Basics with links to indexes

A great place to learn about genealogy research.

OLD COIN AREAS

By far, this is the most requested target class for most detectorists. In all my presentations and speaking gigs, this one gets the lion's share of the attention. Therefore, I'll give it the most thought.

Coin hunts rank high amongst the beginner and intermediate enthusiasts mainly because the success rate of a new hunt is high and the results come quickly. Cache hunting is more advanced, and it may take you a couple of years to hit one. Locate a coin-hunting area, and you get feedback within an hour that your research was good or bad.

Fairgrounds, race tracks, soccer fields, football bleachers, dog races, cock fights, swimming holes—they all are crowd-based coin aggregators. A festival atmosphere with money changing hands will deposit many a coin in the soil. Your job is to find these coin-rich areas and recover them.

Because this is the main focus for 90 percent who are reading this book, I'm going to individually list off all the areas that should be productive to you.

And because you are more advanced than other treasure hunters, I want to emphasize an important concept, the Big Four, pointed out by Dick Stout in his book Where to Find Treasure!

When evaluating the following list, bear in mind the Big Four, especially the last one: What, Where, When, and How Long. These are your new best friends; attend to them and they will treat you well.

What – What is the event? Does it generate a lot of coins on the ground in certain areas or statistically spread out over the entire region?

Where – Location is where? Is that area still accessible? Private or public land?

The Big 4 – When, What, Where, and How Long – are your friends. Pay attention to them, and they will be good to you.

When – During what era of the past did this event occur? Is it pre-1964? Pre-1933? What possible goodies might be on location? Keep your eye open for silver era-targets. (Obviously gold would be good, but finding a gold coin can spoil you for life!)

How Long - How Long was the event there? Was it a county fairground for 40 years? Or a senior class picnic area for three years back in 1972-75? Clearly, you want to give higher priority to long-term areas.

TIER 1 – BEST PERFORMING

Old Schools – Kids are kids. Nothing changes. Kids lose coins, as we all know. Schools are a bit easier to research, yet a bit harder to find sometimes.

There is an emotional attachment to schools we attend, either good or bad. Because of that, every county history book I've ever read covers the old schools. They may not give good locations, but they speak of them. So the trick will be to find the primary sources and figure out where they stood. Schools less than 100 years old are easier to find. Those over 100 years old are a bit tougher.

Look for old topographic maps from the state and from the USGS. The schools are often on these. Old plat maps at the courthouse may also show school locations. The historical society may have reference books on old local schools you have never heard of, so give them a call. If all you have is a general area, find the local historian and ask them. As a last resort, find the oldest aerial photograph you can find at the USGS and try to spot soil marks on the photograph. Old buildings darken the soil.

Old Churches – Churches are social meeting halls, and often buildings were cross adapted—the school was a church, the church was the meeting hall, the meeting hall was a church. So expect coins around a church. Take care to seek out old trees as people congregated in the shade before and after services.

Fairgrounds – Lots of activities, noise, vendors, and money changed hands at the fairgrounds. These can be excellent areas for coin shooters and their locations were usually well documented. Most importantly, they occurred over and over again in the same place, depositing more and more coins on the ground.

Look in local history books, newspaper archives, and historical society archives, and talk to old timers.

Carnivals – Carnivals are a bit trickier than fairgrounds as these are often traveling affairs where they simply set up on open ground outside of town. You may find hints of these in old newspaper archives, personal memoirs, or by talking to old folks in retirement centers. In the newspaper, look at the ads as you may spot dates and places announcing where the carnival will happen. It's unlikely that you can spot anything in the county history books or on old topo maps, but give it a try.

Farmers Markets – Communities sometimes host farmers markets on a regular basis, for example, the first Saturday of the month. These were markets where money changed hands and certainly got lost.

Look in the old newspaper archives because these events recurred on a regular basis. Local historians and the historical society may know their locations. I'd even ask some old folks on the street. It's unlikely to be in a history book as these were not really newsworthy from a historic standpoint.

Military Camps and Bases – Because these locations were occupied, there will be a concentration of coinage. Add to that the bonus of buttons and buckles, and you have a winning target. Do be careful about UXO (Unexploded Ordinance—bombs, hand grenades, i.e. Boom! . . . Where did my left leg go?) The good news is that UXO is rarely found near barracks and administration buildings. Those bases that had UXO areas generally had them cordoned off, and you shouldn't be able to get to them. That applies to the United States; other countries are a different matter. Be wise, stay alive.

The other nice aspect of military locations is that they are well documented, either by the government or by military memoirs. Normally, you can find out precisely how long a camp was occupied and a map of the buildings in the camp.

Your mantra should be "Time on Target." Focus your efforts on camps where troops stayed for 20 years and not so much on camps where troops stayed two months.

Resources would be historic archives of the Department of Defense and the US Archives, *www.archives.gov*. You want to find out the occupation of the base, the layout of the base, how it changed over time, and if any UXO is somewhere down-range on the base. Remember, it may have ended over 150 years ago, but there are still casualties from the Civil War, and those people are all metal detectorists.

Dog and Horse Racetracks – These are similar to athletic fields but with a wildcard—gambling. There will always be a group who wants to gamble on the outcome of a dog or horse race. Local to me, I've heard of several gold Mexican coins that were found at a racetrack nearby.

For resources, you may try old newspapers, the historical society, or old USGS topographic maps. If the racetracks existed after 1940, they may show up in historical aerial photographs.

Old Ports – Old ports saw lots of people moving about in a hurry, with vendors hawking wares and busy sailors with very little shore leave. Coins get lost and stay lost. Old ocean ports are one thing, but river ports are a different beast altogether. While most ocean ports have become concrete jungles, river ports can be a farm field today. Study your history and seek out the long-lost riverbank ports of call. Remember, rivers move, and the old port bank could now be half a mile inland.

Leads should be found in old county history books, newspaper archives, or the local historical society. Excellent leads for seaports will be on US coastal surveys.

TIER 2 – THEY PERFORM, BUT NOT AS WELL AS TIER 1.

Old Hotels and Stage Stops – Any hotel that is 100 years old becomes a very interesting target. Unlike modern hotels that are sterile and whose guests rarely mingle, old hotels were much more engaging businesses where patrons had more opportunities to buy things at the bar, play a game of chance, and drop pocket change around the grounds. If the hotel owner lived on site, you should research to see if a cache is likely.

The life of the hotel is important when determining the priority of the target. Obviously, a hotel or stage stop that was in business 60 years is a more attractive target than one that lived only five years.

To find such hotels, you have a two-step process:

1. Discover the existence of the hotel, then

2. Locate the hotel.

You may find oblique references to them in county history books, in old photographs from yearbooks, or in the archives and photos of the local historical society. Also, you might find ads for them in the newspaper archives at one of the following libraries: historical society, local, or state archive. Because of economics, most hotels should show up in Sanborn maps or other fire maps.

Athletic Fields – Soccer fields, baseball diamonds, football stadiums, etc. distribute coinage in a pattern around the concession stands and bleachers. Your research should focus on where the concession stands stood and then on the seating area. Be aware that the concession stands may have relocated over time.

This isn't listed as a Tier 1 location because the bleacher area can be so junky that it can render the target worthless. Be prepared to use your smallest coil, if you find an old site with lots of trash targets.

The resources that will serve you well are old school yearbooks and old archived newspapers. Look through the yearbooks to find pictures of the ball field which will help you spot the concession stands. Also, take note of trees as these trees may still be standing. Trees can really help crack a case and help you get precise locations—within 10 feet. I will repeat that wonderful tidbit over and over.

Rodeo Arenas – Same as Athletic Fields, see above.

Train Stations – There are scheduled train stations, and there are flag stations. A flag station is a minor train stop that may not have much of a building structure, if any. These weren't true train stations but minor stops where passengers had to raise the flag to be picked up. Many a detectorist has thought of old train stations, I expect, but few would know about flag stops.

Abandoned train stations that are long gone would be ideal targets if the location can be found again.

Major train stops are likely to be one per city. These will likely be known or could be found on a Sanborn map, old topographic map, or in the historical society archives. An online search of the historical train society may reveal forums that you can join and carefully scan for information. If the forum doesn't have that info, you could politely pose the question as a researcher. Train schedules may also appear in the old newspapers, so seek out newspaper archives. And of course, see if the current rail-road owner has an archive as well. Union Pacific has extensive amounts of track and assets. They also were responsible for surveying a huge swath of the West. I expect their archives, if available to the public, to be phenomenal.

The Union Pacific Historical Society (*www.uphs.org*) has a good amount of information in its archives. Plus, they are linked with other railroad historical societies.

Central Pacific Railroad Photographic History Museum
Chicago & North Western
M.K.T (KATY)
MOPAC Missouri Pacific Historical Society
Rock Island Technical Society
Southern Pacific Historical & Technical Society
The Rio Grande Modeling & Historical Society
Western Pacific

Pioneer Camping Grounds – There were areas for pioneers to pitch tents and make a temporary camp. Usually, these were near a source of good water and had some protective features. These camping grounds, or layover camps, have been reported to be very productive. The source for your leads on this solely resides in local county history books.

Revival Meetings – In the 1930s, there was a big surge of revival meetings. These were community events that drew lots of people into fields and pastures, with the event often held underneath tents. It is up to you to find out where these revivals took place.

Look in the local history books then inquire with the historical societies. You might even get lucky if you find an old timer who remembers where these things were.

Chautauqua – Few are still around who know what these were. They started out in 1874 as religious training grounds by Lake Chautauqua. The summer camp was for families and meant to "educate and uplift." The idea caught on, and other Chautauquas, also known as assemblies, sprang forth throughout the country, often taking root in groves of trees by a lake. Within a decade they had evolved and become informational, educational, and inspirational events, sometimes to a point of vaudevillian. Via a circuit, popular performers of the day would visit most of these assemblies.

According to Charlotte Canning, who wrote a report of Chautauquas for the University of Iowa's website, over 10,000 communities in 45 states had Chautauquas. While I've never heard of this event, I'm sure I'm not alone. My wife, however, remembers her grandmother was involved in one.

The Chautauqua circuit mostly collapsed in the Great Depression, and few survived to see the Second World War, likely because of competition from other entertainment mediums like radio and film.

But Chautauquas had great pull, and some big names would bring in lots of people. Lectures were the apparent backbone of the entertainment draw, and some names you might recognize were on the lecture circuit, such as the likes of William Jennings Bryan.[4]

To find these assembly locations, seek out your local historian, cultural heritage society, local historians, and at worst, check the newspaper archives—these were news! A local history book may describe them, but you'll be lucky if they mention

---

4. "W.J. Bryan wasn't a terribly fun fellow. He is infamously known for Anti Evolution, Anti Gold Standard, and Anti Alcohol. How he became a popular speaker is beyond me."

where they were held. I've even found a few witnesses who still remember these as kids.

Fourth of July Picnics – This is self-explanatory. Lots of people went to these picnics because 100 years ago, there wasn't much else for competing entertainment.

Look in newspaper archives for the issue before July 4; this should be a quick search. The historical society may be helpful as well. Be on the alert that the location of the picnic likely changed throughout the decades. Also, if it was at the edge of the woods, the tree-line will drift over time.

Ghost Towns – Here we are talking about a town that faded away and maybe has only a few residents left behind. If you search around the buildings, you'll find some coins but not a great deal of them. However, you do have a shot at a random jackpot cache and the occasional non-metallic antique thingamabob.

There are many books in print about ghost towns. Buy one. I think the main research source for these books is post office records, so they can miss smaller hamlets that are now ghost towns. I'd also recommend you research backwards and look into cemeteries in order to find ghost towns. People aren't usually buried in a large cemetery in the middle of nowhere; they are usually interred near the edge of a population center.

Be sure to enjoy the time spent on your hobbies because you aren't getting out of this life alive.

TIER 3 – LOW-PERFORMING ZONES

You may be better off passing these up unless you have upside points like

a) they are very close to home (low time cost); or

b) there's a chance to find a cache; or

c) there's a chance to find gold coins or jewelry; or

d) there's a chance to find very old coins; or

e) they have low, low junk levels, and hunting is easy and pleasant.

But in general, your time is valuable. If you are going to spend time researching, prepping, and hunting a new location, you should be hunting for a Tier 1 or 2. Remember, it requires the same amount of effort to research a Tier 1 as a Tier 3.

Old houses – Yes, you may protest that these are supposed to be ideal research targets. Well, that is baloney. Pure and simple. Why would a house be a great target? Crowds didn't drop coins there, people didn't lose their change in the roar of the festival trying to buy hot dogs, and there weren't throngs of people having a picnic. It is just a homestead with lots of junk and very few coins. Sure, you will have some kids drop some coins as they hang upside down in a tree, but not many. The only thing this target has going for it is if it is really, really old and you are shooting for barber, seated, or older coinage.

Glen Carson, who wrote the coinshooting series of books, had strong feelings about coin hunting houses. He believed folks really didn't lose much change there because money didn't change hands, so few opportunities existed to lose some. Yes, you may find the odd coin there, but a house is a secondary target, a consolation prize that you can hunt if you find an old house near your primary target.

The main redeeming fact is that houses are the most likely structures to have a cache.

Drive-in Theaters – There will be some coinage lost here, but people stayed mainly in their cars, and if coins dropped, they hit paved ground. The only good hotspot would be the 500 square feet around concessions. This is a bias of the author—there are some who disagree with me and think this is a Tier

1 coin target. Having people challenge your opinion is a good thing. Now prove it to me.

Modern Schools – Modern schools are good for beginners, but not advanced detectorists. If you are lucky, you might find a gold ring. Modern schools are training grounds for detectorists. If you like finding clad coins, this isn't the book for you.

CACHE

Essentially, cache hunting is looking for a buried stash of money that was never recovered by its owner, usually because of the owner's sudden demise or forgetfulness in old age. To be a good cache hunter, you first should understand why caches exist.

Banking is a fairly new invention in civilization. Many still don't trust it. Having seen two banking collapses, I'll step up and say I'm also one who doesn't trust them very much. The Italians invented modern banking in the 1300s, and if you showed up at the bank and they couldn't give you your money, bad things happened. The depositors tended to drag those bankers into the streets and kill them. Ahh . . . Some of us still pine for the old ways.

Back in the fledgling United States, banks weren't within a reasonable distance to do typical banking, nor were they insured by the US government, so many folks didn't use them. They often hid their money instead.

The famous post-hole bank is a side effect of the lack of a nearby, reliable, or trusted banking facility in the region. Putting money in the ground was a great backup plan.

Post-hole banks are the quintessential mason jars filled with silver dollars and buried under fence posts, usually within sight of the bedroom window and at a depth less than three feet as that is the length of a man's arm reaching into a hole.[5]

Now, I've got news for you. People die. It is a fact that we can't avoid that endgame part of life. However, it does leave opportunities in its wake.

For treasure hunters, an opportunity arises when someone passed away unexpectedly, and the heirs, if any existed, didn't find or even know about the deceased's money. This happened quite a bit more than you would think. Consider one small community over the course of 300 years, which covers 10 generations or more, and statistically a few people will have placed deposits in the earth that are not recovered.

Many hidden hoards are stumbled upon by detectorists, but very few by research. Several are discovered by a chance meeting with a plow. Our cousins in Europe have this happen far more than we.

Quite a few were found by soldiers digging trenches, which is how the Hildesheim treasure was found in 1868. In WWI, by the nature the conflict, many a hoard was accidentally found digging trenches.[6]

---

5. Bear in mind, ground level can change dramatically over time. Some areas I worked added three feet of overburden due to erosion uphill from them. I spent three years visiting that area and sampling overburden while digging over 1,000 holes. The average overburden was 23 inches. Oh, and yes, we found our targets.

6. The Romance of Treasure Trove, C.R. Beard, p. 12 - "At that time [summer of 1918] the entire countryside about the little town and Landguard Fort was scarred with trenches. . . . In the process of digging a practice trench on this spot an urn containing between two and three hundred Roman coins was brought to light."

Tyrian coins deposited in first century BC. Caches have
been a viable option for thousands of years. This one
found by archaeologists under an ancient doorway.

One trend that greatly improves your odds of finding a cache
is war. The dangerous times and uncertainty caused by an
invading army greatly increase the number of people who bury
wealth. Any student of troves in Great Britain can attest to
this.[7,8]

There are caches put down by organizations, councils, militaries, bandits, temples, churches, governments, and others, but
by far the most common one found is an individual's cache.

---

7. Buried British Treasure Hoards by Ted Fletcher
8. The Romance of Treasure Trove, 1933 by Beard

Four tons of silver in a cache found in India, apparently hidden from the British during the last century. Research didn't find this; a building renovation crew did. However, research did uncover news of this hoard and via deep web assets we found this image. Does this image help vet the story and corroborate the sources? How much information is in this photo? Photo credit: PTI, fair use.

If you research for wealthy persons who met a sudden death, your odds go up quite a bit. Old newspaper obituaries are very good for this kind of research as they mention murders and facts of the victim's life that can become leads.

PROHIBITION

Prohibition-era rum runners and criminals made a great deal of money. So did moonshiners. That doesn't mean they kept it—people tend to spend easy money fast. However, it does make for a logical target to pursue.

You can focus not only on the Prohibition caches, but also on their copper equipment as sometimes the law caught up to the stills and destroyed them. The law, however, would leave the wrecked still, and often I've heard that the copper from the stills can still be found. At current prices, it sells for a pretty penny. Not to mention, some artifacts left behind, like crockery, are collectors' items.

Moonshiners and rum runners were well known in the area for their wares. Local history usually remembers it; the local historical society may even have files on these men and women. Tracking down their homesteads can be done using tax rolls, census reports, and property transfer research at the courthouse.

Bigger operations began spilling into organized crime, and you may discover that organized crime learned to launder their ill-gotten gains and used the banking system. So chose targets that likely buried their loot, not laundered it. How to do that? Frankly, I don't know, but I suspect the local history legends will indicate how large their gang was, if they were in a gang at all.

The main focus of Prohibition targets will fall in the 1920s through the 1930s. The activity was illegal, and the rum runners and moonshiners understood that every two-bit crook knew where to find them, so it makes sense that their illicit earnings were hidden.

Research on bootleg targets must start with the local history books as they are very worthy stories. Don't forget that the 1930s census is out to help you identify the correct protagonists in the story. Local newspaper archives may discuss local busts.

The courthouse records will also provide you with clues and leads on who was caught and charged with moon-shining and perhaps may mention their associates. Busts, shootouts, and court orders will put you on the path to many locations.

BATTLEGROUNDS

For relic hunters, artifacts of a bygone era hold some charm. But beware—Civil War munitions still kill people to this very day. I don't care how out of print this book has gotten, there will still be injuries and deaths from unexploded ordnance from past wars. France tracks deaths from WWI munitions yearly, and the last few years have averaged 30 deaths per year.

If you are after relics from more modern wars, take care when digging. Talk to other experienced hunters to learn your trade. I've heard Russian metal detectorists scrape dirt off targets sideways, instead of shoveling down. "Why?" you ask. Well, the partners who survived spread the word about the wrong way to do it. Remember, if you die, you won't be around to buy my other books.

UXO: An Iraqi unexploded shell from 1990 on Kubbar Island, off the coast of Kuwait. Do you really want to detect in this area? Photo Credit: Tom Oates, creative commons license.

The good news? There are many primary and secondary sources to tap into for your research. The military machine also was very good about photo reconnaissance, so you will have good luck finding certain sites—as will your competition.

If you are after Civil War stuff, I'd recommend the Official Military Atlas of the Civil War. It has a collection of wonderful maps and tidbits that can even show where buildings were standing. I believe Barnes & Noble reprinted these maps in the last decade.

All other US wars, from 1812 to the Gulf Wars, are heavily documented with books, and those books list other secondary and primary sources. Those sources are federal and, through the Freedom of Information Act, can be obtained if you're patient.

Soldiers were also quite good at publishing their diaries and memoirs, so these primary sources can be a goldmine of tips and leads.

Your local historical society and state historical society will have a list of books relevant to your area in regards to those wars. This should be your main line for getting leads.

MILITARY BASES AND CAMPS

Buttons, belt buckles, and other baubles. Owning them brings people closer to history. Thus, a collectors' market quickly forms after every war. Usually the underdog side is the most coveted of the two. In the case of the US Civil War, this would be the Confederates. With the First Jewish War, the Jewish freedom coins are coveted. Nothing changes—people collect the underdog.

The target on bases and camps is the relics left behind, typically buttons and coins, plus the odd buckle, bucket, bayonet, bullet, and other hardware that gets left behind.

For leads, look to Tufts University's online portal of 19th century sources found at *www.perseus.tufts.edu.*

Ohio compiled a great deal on Civil War troop movements; you can find it at *ehistory.osu.edu/osu*

Also, try the federal archives and archive.org. Local historical societies will also prove quite helpful.

OUTLAW LOOT

Some just can't get away from the romance of the outlaw era. Research can bring the past much closer, but I consider this branch of treasure hunting the most difficult. The trail is the coldest, the primary sources the fewest, and the aerial imagery is the most useless. Most importantly, you are following a trained law officer who also tried to recover the loot.

If you wanted to hear that this is easy and that you can definitely find outlaw treasure, you've bought the wrong book. I'm here to help you research, not to bullshit you.

Those who are passionate about their interest will enjoy the chase and have a chance. If you think this is simply the easiest treasure to chase down, you are in for a rude awakening.

Resources for such endeavors will test your researching skills. There are plenty of secondary sources, many of which are so biased they are not to be trusted and can even be a liability in your research. You will need to learn how to use microfiche machines to scour old archived newspapers from the time in question. Further, you may need to talk with the courthouse staff about where prosecution records from that time period are kept and how to get access to them. Each state is different about when prosecution records can be opened up to the public, and some states are downright prickly about it.

A less-guaranteed resource may be to find the judge who presided over the trial and seek out the colleges and universities nearby to him. He may have donated his papers to them, and these papers may be in a special collection.

I told you this wasn't going to be easy.

OLD WEST

Ghost towns, mining camps, stage stops, and old legends—this is the stuff that many a history buff seeks.

Research using Old West history books, personal memoirs, and old maps. Don't put much faith in "Ghost Town Guides" as you should do your own homework.

There are many, many resources to find leads for Old West targets. Both local and county historical societies will be helpful in this regard. Because of the romance of the subject matter, there will also be many books on the Old West in your area.

For good leads, be sure to keep a keen eye on their sources and vet the authors and sources meticulously. Primary sources will lead you to the good. Writers of the Old West have a bad habit of merely rehashing each other and not doing proper research on primary sources.

OTHER SPECIALTY TREASURE

By "other" I'm referring to the unusual treasure-hunting target—like finding a movie prop that was used in a popular film. (Can you say Maltese Falcon?) Or a spare shell for a historic Russian space satellite. (Sputnik had several spare shells, and one was sold to a collector I know.)

It was in hunting rare specialty treasure that I developed my research skills and really earned my stripes. I was seeking a rare class of treasure, and reports of early accounts are very hard to identify and to acquire. Eventually, I was forced to learn Deep Web research and good research techniques to obtain the sources I had to have. Some sources were so rare I'd have to fly to university libraries to put my hands on rare books in non-circulating collections. But I got my leads, and occasionally I found the targets.

Ultimately this led to many successful hunts, and many, many more unsuccessful ones. It also led to appearing on local TV occasionally and, to my dismay, on foreign national TV.

In time, I graduated to overseas expeditions to South America, Asia, and Africa, which was a reward in and of itself. Africa has a magic to it that few Americans comprehend until they put boots on the ground there.

Seeking specialty treasure is a challenge that requires you to have a firm understanding of research, of authoritative vetting, and of persistence. Beyond that, I can give you only my encouragement and wish you good luck.

CHAPTER FOUR

PURGING TREASURE LEADS

The good news is that you will acquire dozens of treasure leads quickly, but the bad news is you will acquire dozens of treasure leads quickly. An odd state of contradiction, I know. Let me clarify.

As soon as you start reading your county history books, newspaper archives, and other sources mentioned in this book, treasure leads will pop out. You merely need to recognize them and write them down for later vetting.

There will be so many that you need to take a deep breath, step back, and try to strike off the ones that are least likely to be fruitful. Then begin preliminary research on the rest to try to find reasons to scratch them off the list.

Focus on red flags, and throw out leads if they get a red flag.

You will have too many leads; take time to remove the "iffy" ones.

For example, you may encounter stories of misers, but not all misers have money hidden away. Nor do all misers die leaving a cache behind. Some misers just didn't have money. Local stories of a miser with missing money should get your attention, but you will need to ferret out the reason that the locals thought he had money. If there is no logical reason, discount that lead to a lower level or red flag it. Be prepared, however, for a later tidbit that may explain why that miser did have money.

With cache stories, did the individual have a drinking issue or drug problem? If so, there's probably no cache there, so strike that lead off. Do you have a lead on a man known to gamble too much? Again, that doesn't sound good; strike it off. Did a wealthy cattleman live to a ripe old age? Is there any reasonable evidence that he didn't outlive his money?

You are looking for leads where there is an individual who has money coming in, little flowing out, who had a modest lifestyle followed by a quick fate. So your initial research should look more into striking off leads than finding details on where the house is. This is a point in research called the go/no-go point. You either put the lead on a short list or strike it off. You do this to maximize your precious time.

Often, there may be no written record about lifestyle. This kind of vetting may have to be done in the field interviewing neighbors, or kids and grandkids of neighbors. There will be times, however, when it may be just as easy to search a property as find relevant witnesses. Just roll with it.

The more research you do trying to vet leads, the more new leads you will find. You will be in a constant battle to get rid of leads and boil them down to the top 10 juiciest. You don't have all the time in the world, so prioritize.

CHAPTER FIVE

A PRIMER ON INTERNET SEARCHING

This is probably not the primer you are expecting, so don't skip this as what you read here is quite interesting.

I'm going to explain a little-known fact about the Internet so that you can become a much more efficient researcher. This little fact is about how Google is useless 90 percent of the time. Why? Because 90 percent of the Internet is Deep Web and Google can't index it to show you resources you need. Let me say that again because it is an important concept for you: Google cannot find Deep Web resources.

I'll be covering both the Surface Web and the Deep Web. If you've read books before about searching using the Internet, this will be a new twist for you. I'm not going to hold back any punches. I'm just going to tell it like it is.

A lot of How-To-Research tutorials simply cover the "Well, type in these keywords into Google and . . ." which doesn't get you very far. We have to go beyond that and really dive deeply into the research assets of the Internet.

To be fair, the shallow web does hold some minor resources we need. The Deep Web, however, has many more, and they have higher "authority rank" with us. I'll explain authority rank in depth later in the book.

WHAT IS THE DEEP WEB?

Google just doesn't cut it for good research. It is just a Surface Web search engine. If you have no idea what Surface Web is, you've come to the right place.

The Internet is divided into two parts, Deep Web and Surface Web. If a web page can be seen by an indexing bot—Google, for example—then that is considered Surface Web. If Google can't index it and, as a result, can't display it, it is Deep Web.

Deep Web resources are higher quality, higher authority, and a boon to researchers.

Why should you care? Because Deep Web resources are usually higher quality, higher authority, and a boon to researchers, be they high-energy physicists or treasure-troving cache hunters.

MAXIMIZING SURFACE WEB

There are many search engines, but they all do the same thing. They crawl the web and index what they find. There are a few big ones, like *Google, Yahoo, Bing,* and *Dogpile*. Personally, I'm fond of Zuula.com which searches the big ones and gives the results in one page.

There are many more smaller, boutique search engines that specialize, like *Pipl*, used to locate facts on people, Deeperweb. com, and others. Each has a strength; these should be found and added to your Source Deck.

Almost every search engine uses some form of Boolean logic to help you narrow your search:

- If you wanted to find just keywords on a single site on Google, for example, insert the words "recommended books" on treasurenet.com use [recommended books site:treasurenet.com] (but without the brackets).

- If you want university results, insert an "inurl:" like [Montana historical map inurl:.edu].

- If you want text, use "intext:" like [Montana maps calhoun county intext:commission] which would likely find you a Montana map put out by the historical commission.

- If you want a particular word in the title, use "intitle:" like [mountain biking intitle:jumping] which would locate a page with "jumping" in the title about mountain biking.

- If you want keywords in a specific order, e.g. "Black and Tan" when looking for beer, use quotes, like ["black and tan" beer].

- If you don't want certain words in your results, use a minus sign, no space, and the word. For example, we don't want results for tanning salons, so we use ["black and tan" beer -tanning].

- If you want wildcards, use* like [historical * found using Google earth] which may show us links to historical things Google Earth finds.

DEEP WEB ASSETS

There are hundreds of Deep Web assets, but hundreds of those are not useful to a treasure hunter. I mean, do you really need to look at Pubmed.com, the massive medical search engine? Not likely, but you may want to research if a doctor was publishing after 1986 for some reason.

The biggies which are useful to treasure hunters, I've listed below. A good resource to also draw upon is *www.deep-web.org* where they list over a hundred specialized Deep Web engines. I don't know which one you need for your project; only you will be the one to figure that out. Think creatively and focus on other activities nearby or common construction items of the era.

A good resource to also draw upon is www.deep-web.org where they list over a hundred specialized Deep Web engines.

LIBRARY OF CONGRESS – LOC.GOV

The Library of Congress has an enormous amount of material, collections, maps, and artifacts. One particularly impressive resource is the American Memory collection which contains many things. One category of interest is interviews with elderly folk who lived through historical events. The true scope of the American Memory project is best described from the LOC website:

American Memory is a gateway to the Library of Congress's vast resources of digitized American historical materials. Comprising more than 9 million items that document U.S. history and culture, American Memory is organized into more than 100 thematic collections based on their original format, their subject matter, or who first created, assembled, or donated them to the Library.

The original formats include manuscripts, prints, photographs, posters, maps, sound recordings, motion pictures, books, pamphlets, and sheet music.

One of these sub-collections in the American Memory project is the WPA life history, also described by the LOC website as

These life histories were compiled and transcribed by the staff of the *Folklore Project* of the *Federal Writers' Project* for the U.S. Works Progress (later Work Projects) Administration (WPA) from 1936-1940.

An example of one, from the life of Ms. Oatfield, follows. The interview was conducted January 6, 1939. So the reference to the '60s is about the 1860s.

"The old McNary donation land claim is just down the road a short distance. The old house, the photograph of which I am lending you, was destroyed only a few years ago. In the early '60s a murder was committed there that scared the whole countryside. A woman named Mrs. Hager, two daughters and a son were living in the house. They were supposed to have quite a bit of money hidden away, at least the girls bragged about it. (cont.)"

So you can see why this is a very interesting resource. Just take care to identify the interviewee's bias as they may tend to exaggerate a bit to entertain the person interviewing them.

NATIONAL ARCHIVES - WWW.ARCHIVES.GOV

This government resource collection holds so much material that they claim it would circle the Earth 57 times if printed out. What you should find particularly interesting is documentation on all wars that we have fought and also information on Indian affairs.

Because Deep Web assets don't show up on Google searches, think about what university or online database might contain references to your topic of interest, then search for that university or online database.

Of course they have lots of other stuff, but it will take you more than an hour just to understand the scope of their collection, how very little of it is online and that you will need to go into a regional center to do old-fashioned research. Also, I can tell you it won't cover local, gritty, historical stuff, only large-scale federal events.

SMITHSONIAN - WWW.SIL.SI.EDU

The Smithsonian, our nation's attic, can have useful tidbits from time to time. Check them out over at *www.sil.si.edu* and you may find something very useful in a research hunt.

They have several collections, including an image collection which may be useful when trying to spot locations of buildings.

Overall, this is not a key resource, but it can be helpful.

OHIO STATE UNIVERSITY - EHISTORY.OSU.EDU/OSU

OSU hosts a splendid collection of Civil War documentation on troop movements, camps, letters to HQ, etc.

PERSEUS AT TUFTS UNIVERSITY- WWW.PERSEUS.TUFTS.EDU/HOPPER

The majority of this collection is ancient history, but it also contains some more recent 19th century American history which encompasses the Civil War.

Collections include the Richmond newspaper during the Civil War and hundreds of examples of digitized documentation from that time frame. It's an excellent resource of primary and secondary sources, especially some books that are harder to find, even from libraries.

Some of these scanned sources are quiet memoirs and oblique works from around the time of the Civil War that would take a researcher weeks to months to recognize as relevant sources for a Civil War research project.

HIGHWIRE PRESS - HIGHWIRE.STANFORD.EDU

Stanford supports a searchable catalog of the largest repository of free and fee-based full-text, peer-reviewed content (hint! – high authority) from over 900 different journals.

One of the nifty things you can do is set the time frame of the subject you are researching to the era of interest to you, e.g. 1920-1922. You will pull up interesting periodicals from that time frame.

This is one of those tools that will only be useful if you are imaginative in your search criteria.

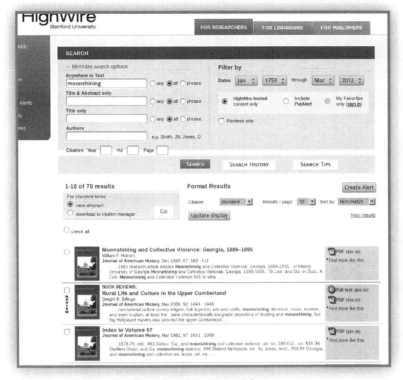

Credit: Highwire Press, fair use.

For example, I searched for "moonshining" and pulled up interesting articles in a periodical called The Journal of American History. However, some articles are full-text free and some are fee based. Now, I'm cheap and don't want to pay for the article, so I'll just write down the issue number and date then see if I can find the full text elsewhere using a Deep Web engine. If I can't find it online, I'll take my shopping list of articles I want with me when I visit my library next. Often my library will have a subscription that lets me see some of these. For the remainder of the articles that I can't find elsewhere, I just have to decide if I want to fork out the cash to buy access to them.

NEWSPAPER ARCHIVES

The larger newspapers, like *The New York Times*, have their archives online, but others are defunct, like the Dallas Times Herald, and have only some issues scanned by local universities. Some may be available via the Library of Congress or at your state library.

Take note, at some point these links below will go bad. This is a book after all. But there will still be sites out there that have access to these old archives. So if they don't work, do a search until you find the archives.

Major newspapers:

> *The New York Times – www.nytimes.com/ref/membercenter/ nytarchive.html* placed their archives online.

> *Chicago Tribune – www.chicagotribune.com* (search for archives)

> *Los Angeles Times – www.latimes.com*

REGIONAL NEWSPAPERS IN THE UNITED STATES AND CANADA

The following is a list of sources with comprehensive lists of nationwide newspaper archives. Some of these links will break over the years, but many of these lists overlap. I believe you should be able to find your newspaper from the links that are still live. Remember, these few links have links to hundreds of newspapers, so don't think I'm cutting you off short on good newspaper archive sources.

Google Newspaper Archives – *sites.google.com/site/ onlinenewspapersite/Home/usa* has ties into the Library of Congress, several universities, city libraries, and other digital collections. It also offers a nationwide list of newspaper archives.

All states and some small towns – *http://www.xooxleanswers.com/free-newspaper-archives/us-state-and-local-newspaper-archives* has links to other sites with links.

Library of Congress Newspaper Archives – *www.loc.gov/rr/news/oltitles.html* is a list of hundreds of United States and Canadian newspaper resources. I hold the LOC in great respect for the quality of the resources they list online.

Ancestry.com – *www.Ancestry.com* (commercial) has newspaper archives and publications available to members. Be sure to check out the Library of Congress first.

University of Penn Newspaper Archive – *gethelp.library. upenn.edu/guides/hist/onlinenewspapers.html* is a useful list of US newspaper archives and dates and looks like a deeper list of Texas newspapers, so this effort may be a deep, comprehensive list.

NewspaperArchive.com – (commercial) is known for a large collection. I haven't used it, so I can't confirm this.

ARCHIVE.ORG

Archive.org is a deep, broad, and awesome resource for researchers. This site is truly an archive of wonderful items of text, sound, and video. It contains everything from the old Edison company's 1900 footage of the Galveston hurricane destruction, to audio interviews of freed slaves, to scans of old, rare history books.

This will be one of the regular resources you will peruse on every history project you undertake. Because all the items in the vast catalog are indexed and tagged, an intelligent search using focused keywords will discover previously unknown books, manuscripts, memoirs, photos, and recorded accounts. Often I had no idea such resources existed; I simply queried for certain words and hit a jackpot of information.

One of the key searches that should be done on any lead generating search is to look for ALL the local history books for a certain county or region. An earlier edition is usually better as the historical accounts are covered in more depth and more names are given to lead you to primary sources. Old county books are a prize, but the true prize on Archive.org is finding an old, published diary. You are seeking the older, out-of-print county history books that your local libraries don't have and can't get. Be warned, many county history books have neither the word "county" nor "history" in their names. For example, a critical book for me was titled Land of Good Water.

It is from recent county history books that you will learn the names of the older books, and from these older books you may learn of even older reference works. There is a chain of progression you must follow. Some of the reference books may be memoirs or books in which history was a peripheral chapter. These can either corroborate some of your research or point you somewhere new. Archive.org helps out in this progression as it may have the older works referenced. Embrace it, for it is your new best friend.

Photos are also available and I encourage you to always search to see if your area of interest has a photo archived here. You will have to be creative with your keywords when you search for photos.

MULTI-SOURCE SEARCH ENGINES

Zuula.com – This is a multi-engine search page. It runs your keyword search across all the major and minor engines.

Deeperweb.com – This engine runs your search via each niche: news, web, resource, blog, image, etc. You merely review the top answers to each niche and choose which subset niche you want. This is quite handy as you will discover that most of the time you were really looking for answers from a certain niche.

Nifty search tool that breaks out the results by source type.

scholar.google.com – Google found a way to tap and index huge chunks of academic papers, but sometimes only the abstract was indexed. So this is more "kind-of-Deep Web" rather than "Deep Web."

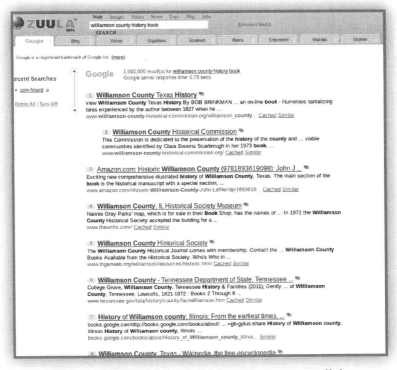

There are multi-search engines that run parallel
searches on several engines at once.

CHAPTER SIX

RESEARCH TOOLS

A NOTEBOOK

Not sexy, but practical. I keep a single notebook for leads. When I spot a lead, I give it a dedicated page. As I flush out the lead and if it fills up the page, I tear the page out and the lead gets its own folder. It's a very simple system, which keeps life easy.

What you don't want to do is have all your leads and your notes on leads in one notebook spread throughout the notebook. One page, one lead. Simple. It may waste paper, but it does save time. Which is more valuable?

WEB BOOKMARKS

Bookmarks are dumb. There is no user data attached to the bookmark to explain what need that bookmark satisfied. You may not even remember why or when you bookmarked that web page. If you have other notes about the web page on why it is useful, you aren't able to attach that info to the bookmarked page. Because of this, we need an intelligent bookmarking tool.

Both Zotero and Evernote fit the bill. Both of these allow you to take notes on the web page, store source information, or any other meta data you want attached. Both Evernote and Zotero even permit online collaboration with partners.

Further, both can bookmark a PDF document, image, or other web-based item.

ZOTERO

Zotero is a plug-in tool that you can add to Firefox or Internet Explorer. It originally was designed as a citation and research aggregation tool for academics that captured the URL and the author and publisher information off the web page to make it easy to cite sources. It evolved and got more powerful. It now is stronger than ever as Zotero is coming out with a standalone program as well as an app for your Droid or iPhone. It also uploads your information and bookmarks to their cloud server which you can access. Most of you will just want the plug-in.

Installation is reasonably easy. In Firefox go to Tools → Add-ons and search for "zotero."

Zotero now is collaborative. You can create a research "group" in Zotero and make it private, public-invite-only, or fully open to the public. If you share, others can see your entries and add bookmarks of web pages, append PDFs, attach images and even videos—all kinds of data can be filed. Then Zotero will index it all so that it can be rapidly found, which is great for large and complex research projects.

As a bonus, because it was originally designed for citation, it can make excellent citations. If you want to publish your work to American Zoology, Mental Health International, or to Studies in the Judean Desert, there are numerous citation formats supported and Zotero will cleanly export your list. For most of us, Chicago Manual of Style will be fine, but many academic periodicals want specific formats.

Zotero works with Windows, Mac, and Linux. Add to that list Android, and I think Apple mobile products, also.

I have high regard for Zotero and encourage you to make this one of your core tools during research. Learn it, use it, love it. A year from now, you will be singing ballads in its honor.

Did I mention it is free? And easy. It takes about 30 minutes to understand most of it. (Or five minutes if you are under 20.)

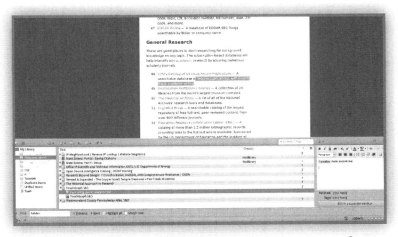

Zotero and Evernote is the next evolutionary stage of bookmarks. Lots of metadata and functionality around a link.

EVERNOTE

Evernote.com is a popular note-taking plug-in for web browsers. They have expanded it to other services, but I'm just going to tell you about the note-taking side. You can surf the web, find an interesting web page, and make a copy of it with a note you write to yourself. You also can tag that note with keywords. Once you make a note, it is uploaded into Evernote's cloud servers and synced with all your other computers that have an Evernote plug-in, so your laptop, desktop, iPad, etc. all have the same notes in them.

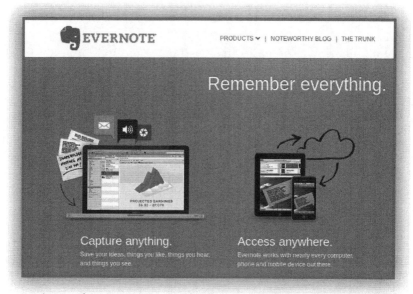

Let's say, for example, you surf to a site about green tea, you spot a funky green tea called "monkey-on-my-back" and you make an Evernote to yourself to buy a pound for your uncle's birthday. You tag the note as "birthday gifts." Two months later, you remember you found some cool things for gifts, you look into your Evernote account, search for "birthday gifts," and you find half a dozen notes to yourself, including the one about this gift idea for your uncle.

You can Evernote pictures, web pages, PDFs (and Evernote pro can OCR the contents for you), and just about anything on the web.

Further, if you have a partner, Evernote can be used collaboratively just like Zotero. You just tell it what folders or notes to be shared with your partner. As long as your partner has Evernote on their computer, they can see the notes you've made and shared.

Drawbacks: Evernote only works on Windows and Mac. As a Linux guy, this was a deal breaker, which is why I chose to go with Zotero.

SOURCE DECK

"What is a source deck?" It is a list of sources, with notes and memos on the nuances of using said sources. This "source deck" is a technique I borrowed from the military; they use it for OSInt (aka Open Source Intelligence) gathering and analysis. Basically it's a listing of all potential sources (i.e. websites on specific topics) of information on any given subject.

Simply put, a source deck is a spreadsheet or word document which lists topics and the websites or resources that have information on those topics. The reason you use a source deck is to avoid repeating the time needed to find good sources. (Remember, your time is valuable!) Plus, you can better describe the resource—its strengths, its weaknesses, your authority ranking for it, and any other tidbits that help define the source.

An example would be a Pentagon weapons analyst on North Korea who notices a new missile on parade from a state broadcast. He immediately would check his internal classified database to confirm it was not previously identified then go to his source deck and find his entries under "missile info" websites (let's say he has four listed, like globalsecurity.org) and begin searching for information or feedback from the sites on this new missile. He finds that two of the missile analysis websites have addressed this new missile. The forums on these two sites have experts who recognized the missile has an impossible control fin and welding flaws and therefore cannot be a working missile. Thus, the weapons analyst has used his source deck to quickly locate highly authoritative website sources which saved him a great deal of time. He writes up his report citing the OSInt from these two websites that the new missile is just another bogus weapon (which isn't surprising as both North Korea and Iran have a habit of inventing and displaying fake weaponry).

A relevant example to a metal detectorist would be in the case where he has discovered some unusual nails. He knows nails are a good aid to help date a site to within a few decades. He also remembers putting nail identification sites in his source deck a couple of years ago.

So when he gets home, he looks in his source deck and locates three websites for square nails:

NAILS

University of Vermont – Basic history of nails going back 1800. *http://www.uvm.edu/histpres/203/nails.html*

Worthpoint – author attributed. Manufacturing history of nails back to 1700s, manufacturing theory of nails. *http:// www.worthpoint.com/blog-entry/tale-nails*

Harp Gallery – author attributed. Identifiable features of nails in furniture, manufacturing for centuries, and discussion of nails going back to 3000 BC. Has photos. *http:// www.harpgallery.com/library/nails.htm*

Mapping and Related Material

GIS For Dummies   http://www.dmos.info/eng/GIS%20For %20Dummies.pdf
Soviet Maps
http://www.sovietmaps.com/index.htm
Maps Of War
http://www.mapsofwar.com/
Maps and Driving Directions   http://www.reverse-lookup.com/maps.htm
Maps and References
http://www.cgrer.uiowa.edu/servers/servers_references.html
CIA World Fact Book
http://www.odci.gov/cia/publications/factbook/
Leading source of land information. Note: Learn to use this one and you'll be quite impressed.

Source Decks save you a great deal of time in searching for highly authoritative information on specific subjects. Over time, your source deck will be long and richly populated.

Another example would be if you were researching oil and gas well information in Texas, you may have spent 30 minutes researching online to discover that the Texas Railroad Commission monitors that data (*www.rrc.state.tx.us*) but the raw data is at Neubus (*http://rrcsearch.neubus.com/esd-rrc/ index.php?_module_=esd&_action_=keysearch#results*).

So you would add two new lines into your source deck under Oil and Gas:

Texas Railroad Commission– *rrc.state.tx.us* (monitors)

Texas RRC actual data– *http://rrcsearch.neubus.com/esd-rrc/index.php?_module_=esd&_action_=keysearch#results* (data, maps, filings)

The way to use a source deck is just to open the source deck and leave it open in the background while you are researching. When you need it, you reference it, and when you find a new source for something, you add that resource so that you never have to hunt for it again.

FREEMIND - MIND MAPPER

Although the term "mind mapping" is a bit odd, the tool itself is very useful. This may become one of your favorite project tools for home projects, research, and work as well, so pay attention to this!

What is a "mind mapping" tool? Well, it is a silly name for an organization tool that lets you outline a project or problem as circles in a visual display. Every fact or aspect you know goes into a circle, and you can drag the bubbles together so that it makes sense. This will make more sense when you see a mind map.

Freemind is one of several "mind mapping" software tools available. Freemind happens to be free, and I use it, so I recommend it.

I use a mind mapping tool when I'm on a big engineering project to understand the relationships. It can also be used in many ways for critical thinking, problem analysis, goal setting, researching, operations management, etc. In our case, it would be useful for every history project.

I also use it when I'm writing a book. The following is my mind map for this book.

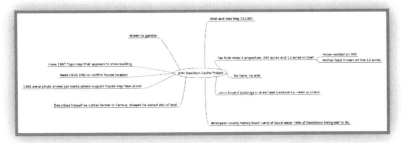

A mindmap is a tool for organizing concepts or tasks.

In terms of a project, you would use a mind mapper to graphically display the information you know about your lead and all the items you want to know about it. This is just a visualization tool to help you understand the scope of the project, what has been done, what needs to be done, and the relationship of all the pieces in the project.

This won't be a tool you will use for every project; only a small percentage of complex projects will need it—especially those where you have partners who need to be briefed on where you are and what you need to do next.

CHAPTER SEVEN

HOW GOOD RESEARCH IS DONE

RESEARCH – 99 PERCENT DON'T HAVE A CLUE

This is about research. Before we even think about Deep Web research, we need to understand research itself.

Before we can go further, we must decide what type of research is to be done. Most people think research is about Googling a topic, and then they are done. While that does provide some useful—and even actionable data—it is an amateurish approach to good research.

GATHERING DATA ON THE SCOPE OF YOUR PROBLEM

Research is about finding facts, vetting those facts, and drawing conclusions. It is also about looking for flaws in your own work and re-evaluating your analysis and conclusions to fix them.

You're neither right nor wrong because others agree with you. You're right because your facts and reasoning are right.

CHOOSING OUR RESEARCH METHOD

The two main methods of research are:

- **Scientific Method** – for analysis of nature and its properties

- **Historical Method** – for systematically investigating a topic

Most may remember the scientific method from high school. The scientific method is used for studying natural science and phenomena. It isn't used for analyzing history, which means it won't be good for treasure-hunting research.

Normally, a treasure lead will cover research about a person, business, place, or event. So we will be focusing on the historical method.

We will use this method to re-create events, understand ties, spot cause-and-effect, and try to get into the shoes of people who lived in a different time. We will use it to identify good sources and throw out bad sources.

Once we've done that, we should be able to draw some conclusions.

Sometimes example conclusions may be:

a.   Given the fellow's lifestyle, likely income stream, and time of year, it is unlikely there was surplus money to make a worthwhile cache.

b.   The army had to ford a river at point X because the horses needed a low-terrain slope and because of the marching fatigue level and enemy pressures.

c.   The paymaster with the army had no reason to believe he was under real threat of capture by the opposing side. Therefore burying a small payroll was more risky than packing it out with the army.

Our conclusions should be sound and survive critical analysis by others. There should be no glaring holes, nor evidence that isn't explained. Conclusions can often bring out red flags on leads which kill off the lead. Not all conclusions will help develop a project; quite often they will be fatal to a lead. Be prepared to be a skeptic.

HISTORICAL METHOD

In a nutshell, we're looking at source material (books, newspapers, eyewitness reports) and trying to corroborate these with each other and with external clues. This method also relies heavily on author authority, which we'll address later.

Wikipedia sums up the historical method nicely:

Core principles [of the historical method]

The following core principles of *source criticism* were formulated by two *Scandinavian* historians, Olden-Jørgensen (1998) and Thurén (1997):

- Human sources may be relics such as a *fingerprint*; or *narratives* such as a statement or a letter. Relics are more credible sources than narratives.

- Any given source may be forged or corrupted. Strong indications of the originality of the source increase its reliability.

- The closer a source is to the event which it purports to describe, the more one can trust it to give an accurate historical description of what actually happened.

- A *primary source* is more reliable than a *secondary source* which is more reliable than a *tertiary source*, and so on.

- If a number of independent sources contain the same message, the credibility of the message is strongly increased.

- The tendency of a source is its motivation for providing some kind of bias. Tendencies should be minimized or supplemented with opposite motivations.

- If it can be demonstrated that the witness or source has no direct interest in creating bias then the credibility of the message is increased.

PROCEDURES

Bernheim (1889) and Langlois & Seignobos (1898) proposed a seven-step procedure for source criticism in history:

1. If the sources all agree about an event, *historians* can consider the event proved.

2. However, majority does not rule; even if most sources relate events in one way, that version will not prevail unless it passes the test of critical *textual analysis*.

3. The source whose account can be confirmed by reference to outside authorities in some of its parts can be trusted in its entirety if it is impossible similarly to confirm the entire text.

4. When two sources disagree on a particular point, the historian will prefer the source with most "authority"—that is the source created by the expert or by the eyewitness.

5. Eyewitnesses are, in general, to be preferred especially in circumstances where the ordinary observer could have accurately reported what transpired and, more specifically, when they deal with facts known by most contemporaries.

6. If two independently created sources agree on a matter, the reliability of each is measurably enhanced.

7.   When two sources disagree and there is no other
means of evaluation, then historians take the source
which seems to accord best with common sense.[9]

PRIMARY VS. SECONDARY SOURCES

A common example of someone with a source problem:

Bob Smith: "Well, my brother's uncle's barber's dog told me
that his other cousin's great-great-aunt's step-cat was once a
sentinel for a KGC hoard of 10,000 pounds of doggie biscuits
and a million gold double eagles from the Confederate
treasury."

George in Accounting: "Actually, according to the study
done by Burdekin and Langdana called "War Finance in the
Southern Confederacy, 1861–1865," printed in Explorations
in Economic History 30 (July 1993), along with several other
credible scholars over the last few decades clearly showed that
massive inflation occurred from lack of gold and silver to back
Confederate notes. The South was dependent upon cotton
for its cash, and, with the blockade, it financially collapsed.
Further, there are no primary source accounts, save one train
trip, of the Confederate government hiding large amounts of
gold. So I heavily doubt that story."

Clearly, some sources are more credible.

While our intuition understands this, researchers have codified
trust and source authority with terminology that is quite help-

9. "Historical Method." The Free Encyclopedia, The Wikimedia Foundation, Inc., 8
JULY 2012, Web.

ful. Researchers break up sources into two groups, primary and secondary. Each is given an intrinsic authority or trust level.

(I'll cover KGC foolishness later.)

PRIMARY SOURCE

Primary source is the information or material chronologically closest to a person, period, or idea being researched, e.g. the recording of the newscaster at the Hindenburg disaster or the daily journal of a soldier.

Do your research well or your project may go down in flames.

Essentially, a primary source is a contemporaneous account of an event or an account by someone who was there.

Another example would be Josephus Flavius, who wrote of the Jewish War in the first century. Part of Jewish War covers history way before his time, but because his work is the only document that covers that history, it defaults as primary source. So a piece of documentation which is the closest to an event is considered a primary source if it is the only source even if it was written years later.

SECONDARY SOURCE

Secondary sources use or cite primary sources and often build upon or extend the interpretation of primary sources, e.g. a book or thesis about the Hindenburg disaster or a biography of a soldier in WW2.

So a secondary source is a writer spotting ideas, theories, or themes from the primary source and secondary accounts. These are often written for commercial gain, like a nonfiction book or an article written for a journal or association. Sometimes they are just written as a summary by a non-academic author to help educate others.

The danger here is that some authors will speculate heavily on their primary sources and write some pretty crazy things. Worse than this is when an author writes an analysis that is based upon only secondary sources, so his work suffers from historical GIGO—Garbage In, Garbage Out. The author is just expanding on errors of errors in many cases.

Wikipedia is a collection of secondary sources and may cite primary sources. Wiki in and of itself is never considered a primary source. Wiki often gives clues to where primary sources should be found, e.g. "Black Bert killed a slave in Calhoun County in 1832 and was tried." (citation of Calhoun trial records) Therefore, you would look up prosecution records in Calhoun County on Black Bert. Court prosecution records would be considered primary sources.

In practice, assume you are researching a Civil War era Texas cavalry unit. There are plenty of secondary sources like Old West books. There are some primary sources, like published diaries of the men, and some published military orders and ephemera in the congressional War of the Rebellion series. These were written for public consumption in a politically charged atmosphere where the winning side must appear to have the moral high ground. We will have to consider bias in those primary sources, but we'll address that next after this quick test.

A TEST ON CATEGORIZING SOURCES

Now it's time for you to test your understanding of sources.

I found a rare book while searching Archive.org on local Texas history for Houston. In the book, Harris County, 1822-1845, written by *Looscan, Adele Lubbock Briscoe* sometime between 1903 and 1935, she put into her first page the following sources:

> "Original letters and business papers of the family of John R. Harris, of Lewis Birdsall, and of Andrew Briscoe;"

- These would be primary sources; letters and papers usually are.

> "records of county court, probate and commissioners courts, and district court of Harris county;"

- Court documents are almost always primary sources.

"The Gazette, published at San Felipe de Austin, October, 1829. by Goodwin Brown Cotton;"

- This sounds like a newspaper, so it probably is a primary source, but may be secondary if it is repeating another paper's news. Beware of bias.

"The Telegraph and Texas Register (Houston), 1838-1856 (incomplete)"

- Sounds like a newspaper. See above

"The Morning Star (Houston), volumes 1 to 6, 1839-1844;"

- Sounds like a newspaper. See above

"'Extracts from an Historical sketch of Harris County,' by C. Anson Jones, in Burke's Texas Almanac, 1879, taken from an address read by him at the centennial celebration held at the State Fair Grounds, in Houston, July 4, 1876,"

- This sounds like a derivative work of a secondary source. Discount heavily.

"'A Manuscript History of the Early Settlement of Harris County,' by Mrs. Mary J. Briscoe (only daughter of John R. Harris written by her for the Ladies' Reading Club of Houston in 1885;"

- Unless she is writing about current history, this is a secondary source.

"The Morning Star, H. D. Fitch, editor, Houston, March 4, 1840;"

- Sounds like a newspaper. See above

"Letters from A. B. Dodson of Alice, Texas,"

- Primary.

"Texas Almanac, 1858, pp. 115-116, and 1859, pp. 36-59, From Virginia to Texas (1835), being a diary of Colonel Wm. F. Gray, published by A. C. Gray in 1909;"

- This sounds like a son publishing his father's diary. Diaries are almost always considered primary if written by contemporaneous people to the event.

"Six Decades in Texas, by F. R. Lubbock,"

- Probably secondary.

"'Troubles of a Mexican Revenue Officer,' by Eugene C. Barker, in The Quarterly, IV, 190-202;"

- This sounds like a primary, assuming it is autobiographic.

"'Reminiscences of Mrs. Dilue Harris.' Ibid., IV, 85-127, 155-189, VII, 214-222;"

- This could be primary or secondary depending on author and account. Likely it's primary; however, it's written long after the events, so discount.

  "'The first Texas Railroad,' by P. Briscoe, Ibid., 279-286;"

- Secondary account likely, unless the author worked on the railroad at the time in question.

  "Year Book for Texas by C. W. Raines; "

- Probably secondary.

  "Biographical (1901) sketches by John Henry Brown, in his Indian Wars and Texas Pioneers;"

- This sounds like a secondary source.

  "Biographical sketches of citizens of Houston and Galveston in History of Texas, published by Lewis Publishing Company, Chicago, 1895."

- This sounds like it outlines the characters of Houston and Galveston, and it may be the earliest record of some of them. So this book could be either primary or secondary. We don't know yet.

  "'A Tale of Two Texas Towns' (Anahuac and Harrisburg), by Adele B. Looscan;"

- Hang on, isn't this the same lady that wrote the book we're examining? I think it is. If this is a history book, it is a secondary source. If it covers current town tales, it may be primary. You'll just have to read it and find out.

"Galveston News, September 6, 1903."

- Sounds like a newspaper. See above

"'History of The Texas Press,' by A. C. Gray, in A Comprehensive History of Texas, II, 368-423,"

- This sounds like a secondary source.

"and copies of papers filed in court in the succession of John R. Harris, the final settlement of the business having been effected by Judge Andrew Briscoe."

- This is a primary source, high authoritative score.

"The 'Extracts from an Historical Sketch of Harris County,' were, so far as statements about early settlers are concerned, chiefly obtained from John Liams (son of the first settler), and members of other families who arrived at an early period."

- This sounds like this is now a primary source compiled by a third party.

Overall, the book Ms. Briscoe has written is a well researched secondary source.

VETTING INFORMATION

We've talked about primary sources, now about vetting the information. We will get information from several sources during our research, so we need to rank that qualitatively somehow.

For example, if we want to know the physical location of the building where John Doe lived in 1944, a property tax search would find the address of 101 Main Street, Tinytown, Texas. (Primary source #1)

Google Maps gives us a location on a map of (Location A). Yet, MapQuest (Secondary source #1) gives us (Location B) and the census address shows (Location B). However, an old photo (Primary source #2) shows no buildings at either (Location A) or (Location B), but a building 100 yards south of (Location B) looks like a good candidate that we'll call (Location C).

While on site getting ground truth, you chat up an old timer (Primary source #3) who says, "John? Ya, he lived in the red brick building over yonder where that chimney now lies on its side," which happens to be about (Location C) where the building was in the photo. Hopefully, your instincts are telling you more authority should be given to the old timer's location than MapQuest, but why?

Common sense is trying to tell you to trust the old timer (Primary source #3). Also, your brain is processing the fact that MapQuest (Secondary source #1) addresses will not line up with 60-year-old postal addresses because it isn't contemporaneous to the time frame in question.

Instinctively, you know to trust primary sources over secondary. I'm just formalizing that fact with this example. We're going to cover this in more depth and call it what it is – Authority Rank.

CHAPTER EIGHT

INTRO TO AUTHORITY RANK OR "SHOULD I TRUST THAT GUY?"

WHEN I USE THE WORD "AUTHORITY," I MEAN IN TERMS OF TRUST.

There is an old adage, "Don't believe anything you read and half of what you see." This is an extreme view, but it expresses the sentiment that you should somewhat distrust the written word. We are not going to be that extreme; we need to be much more intelligent and not group all written word into a simple binary "Trust/Don't Trust" status. Instead, as a good researcher, we will make a varying score on the source's authority.

Example 1 – Website XYX:

For example, let us say we find a website about Jesse James that says he didn't really die in a gunfight but lived to be 100 and ran a secret society called the Knights of the Golden Circle (KGC). There is no author given. The website is on a free blogging website that anyone can create. There are no citations of sources for this extraordinary claim. On a scale of 1 to 10 (10 being high authority), how would you rank the authoritative-ness of this website? I'd put it at a 1 because it stinks worse than eight-day-old fish.

Example 2 – Rebel Gold Book:

Now, how about the book Rebel Gold? It discusses hunting Confederate gold that was allegedly given to the KGC who buried it in elaborate fashion with complex mapping and established an onsite sentinel system to guard it until the Confederate cause rises again to succession. So essentially, dirt poor hillbillies who belong to a secret society guard a multi-million dollar treasure for a cause long dead. We know the author's name, and there are a few erratic references to some sources. How would you rank the authority of this book? Does the premise pass muster for common sense?

If you ranked this low, there is hope for you. The author shows no believable scholarly treatment of his extraordinary claims, has no background in history, and the conclusion doesn't pass common-sense muster. (The book, however, does make for a fun read if you don't mind the gaping holes.)

Example 3 – A University Website:

What if Brainiac University had a web page that discusses the history of the hot springs resorts in a five-county area of Arkansas? This website explains that several hot springs resorts shut down and went out of business in the Depression because of the economy. It gives dates of operations for these resorts and cites the source data for the conclusions. We know the name of the author, who appears to be a grad student in the history department. Does this premise pass muster? How would you rank the authoritativeness of this website?

If you ranked it fairly high, then you agree with me. I gave it high marks because it makes sense, there is little bias and no agenda, and the author vets out to be a known researcher. This doesn't mean he's right, but it does mean I give him higher authority than average.

Example 4 – Genealogy Website XYZ:

This site discusses several lives of Texas Rangers in the 1870s. One of interest to you is of Bob "Crooked Shot" Huffy. The author reports Huffy served in the 23rd "Bad Shot" company in Upton County, Texas, from November 1872 to March 1874. There is mention that Huffy served at an outpost on the south bank of the Yegua River near the intersection of the military road. The author's name is known and is a contributing amateurish genealogist. The website appears to be a for-hire website, not a free one. Citations include payslips of Huffy's and some books. Does the fort story pass muster? How would you rank the authoritativeness of this website?

If you graded this one mediocre, I'm proud of you. First, a quick map check will show there is no Yegua River or even creek in Upton County. Fort locations in Texas are mostly known, albeit a few outposts may not be known. The author is given higher than average authority, but I think he may be off on his stories on the fort. He is most likely confusing stories or propagating errors from history books. Fortunately, we can pull his sources and find out the truth. If he propagated an error in a book, it was because he didn't vet his sources or he failed to give proper authoritative weight to certain authors.

These examples were just an introduction; we really have to judge primary sources differently than secondary. So let us do that next.

AUTHOR'S BIAS IN PRIMARY SOURCES

Every author has a bias. Including me. As an intelligent reader, your job is to identify and remove the bias in your analysis of the primary or secondary source.

A soldier writing in his personal diary the day after a battle to tell the grim and bloody tale of what happened will have the bias of his side of the story. It will also be a fresh rendition of the event and likely be very close to the truth.

That same soldier writing a letter home to his wife a week later will have another bias, most likely a softened version so that he doesn't scare his wife.

That same soldier writing a memoir for publication about the battle three years later will have a greater bias as he needs to cater to a larger audience to sell his book.

In all three cases, notice that the soldier does not have a malevolent, conspiratorial bias. Also notice each case is still a primary source. The bias is present because of the social norms he lives under. He may not even be aware of the bias he puts into each of his accounts. It is this innocent bias that we must always be aware of, and we must discount the source appropriately.

Once you understand the bias of the author and the authority he imparts on his work, you can better use your judgment to accept some of the story, part of the story, or none of the story.

VETTING AUTHORS OF SECONDARY SOURCES - ADVANCED

NOTE! This section doesn't apply to primary sources, only to secondary.

This chapter discusses a very advanced technique. If your head hurts, skip this and go to the next chapter. Just understand the concept of spotting low quality research.

Vetting of authors of secondary sources is a bit more complicated. Secondary source authors are analyzing, interpreting, and deconstructing events reported by primary sources to find patterns, and then they tell you their conclusions as if they were fact. Sometimes secondary sources just extrapolate their favorite theories and pet peeves and present them as divine canonical works from above. You must be on the lookout for a dusting of bullshit, partial bullshit, or full-on steaming bullshit.

In the case of books, there is always the bias to make the book sellable. This is why treasure books are so untrustworthy as research sources.

For the evaluation of secondary-source authors, I just look for specific things and mentally add and subtract bonuses to their scorecard in my head. However, I will try to quantify it for those of you who want to try to understand how I evaluate my secondary-source authors. I've broken it down into a scorecard method. Authority Rank Scorecard Method:

+6 if author is known to publish in peer-reviewed scholarly journals

+5 if written with citations that go to primary sources or +2 for secondary citations

+3 if article is hosted on a government or university's website (.gov or .edu)

+2 if article is hosted by a reputable news media (e.g. NY Times, Washington Post)

+2 if author publishes other articles in non-peer-reviewed journals

+2 if author publishes contact mailing address

+1 if author publishes contact email

+1 if article appears written for a scholarly audience

+2 if article originates from government report (modern or vintage, doesn't matter)

-1 if article refers to any "they" as a vague Illuminati

-2 if article hosted on a "free" web-hosting or blog site like xxxxxx.blogspot.com

-4 for no author name given to an article (no penalty for government report/police report as they are sometimes authorless reports)

-4 if writing is poorly organized or there are spelling and grammatical errors, all suggestive of superficial thinking and research

Start all articles with a default "5" score and add the bonus or penalty from there.

How to interpret the total:

- **3 or below:** The author is to be almost ignored; don't let them walk your dog, let alone tell you history.

- **4–7:** The author may have some credibility, but be cautious.

- **8–14:** It is safe to put faith in the author's credibility.

- **15 and up:** Believe them.

Of course, you should check some of the cited sources. If they turn out bogus, meaningless, or inappropriate, that is a major penalty. If I were to put a number on it, I'd say -7. An author that references bad work clearly wasn't researching well or wasn't able to evaluate and identify crap. This is why I discredit "treasure sign" books which cite other known-bad "treasure sign" books. Garbage in will only get you garbage out.

If you really, really get into source authority, you may want to see the five levels of authority that the *Journal of the Association for History and Computing* (JAHC) has developed. Just Google "JAHC authority levels" or see the following link:

http://quod.lib.umich.edu/j/jahc/3310410.0007.204?rgn= main;view=fulltext

SOME VETTING EXAMPLES OF SECONDARY SOURCES

Example 1 – Book

Spanish Expeditions into Texas by Foster, bibliography with over 100 books, 200+ footnotes, written by a self-appointed county historian

Grade = 14 = 5 + 5 (primary sources) + 1 (scholarly audience) + 3 (a university press publication) This is a very trustworthy author, even as an amateur, but he still can make mistakes.

Example 2 – Website

www.outlawtreasure.worldbreak.com/about.html covers the wonders of KGC treasure, has author name and email, plus mailing address, no references, hosted on a free web host, has grammatical errs and disorganized layout

Grade = 2 = 5 + 2 (author address) + 1 (author email) - 2 (free hosting) – 4 (disorganized) Conclusion - Do not trust this author to give any useful analysis. The only useful thing he might provide is a hint at another source to be investigated.

Example 3 – Book

Tales from the Red River Country by Butts, published off a printer with a comb binding. Purchased at the Red River clerk's office who allowed the local historian to unofficially pedal the county history book. Contains multiple citations, primarily of newspapers.

Grade = 6 = 5 + 5 (primary sources) - 4 (disorganized, amateurish)

The analysis may be off. This author clearly means to be accurate and has no detectable bias. His research just doesn't seem deep as he heavily leans on newspaper accounts. It also isn't polished which means it was a fast job and may have missed things. Still, it is useful.

Example 4 – Web Article

The Texas State Historical Association's website on Texas moonshining history has the author's name but no contact info. The author wrote an article as well in the East Texas Historical Journal which is not quite peer reviewed and has five books listed in the bibliography which all appear to be secondary sources.

Grade = 12 = 5 + 3 (hosted on a state agency website) + 2 (published in an academic journal, non-peer-reviewed) + 2 (kind of cites secondary sources)

In conclusion, this author has high credibility. Although this is a layman's article written by an academically inclined author, he has academically published. I have concern that all his sources are secondary, however.

DEPARTING THOUGHTS ON EVALUATING SECONDARY AUTHORS

Having a high grade does not imply that the author can walk on water; it merely means they have made the cut that weeds out cranks and half-baked researchers.

With that said, I'm going to move on to the good stuff . . . mapping and aerial imagery research.

CHAPTER NINE

MAP RESOURCES

If you skipped the other chapters just to get to this one, I understand. And clearly, you understand the value of maps. Just be a good boy or girl and read the other chapters later.

The focus of this chapter is finding meaningful aerial imagery, satellite imagery, and maps. There is a big difference between a map and aerial imagery. Maps are created from disparate information, while aerial and satellite imagery are photographs taken while looking down from the sky.

Maps can come in a huge array of forms, such as topographic maps, 7.5-minute quadrangle maps, survey maps, or plat maps. Each map will tell a story of the relationship among features on the landscape. Bear in mind, every map you've ever seen is wrong. There is always intentional and unintentional errors that creep into the map-making process. Don't blindly assume that just because the map came from XYZ, it is correct.

> ### *All maps are wrong, most maps are useful.*
> – OLD CARTOGRAPHIC PROVERB REFERRING
> TO THE FACT THAT THERE ARE ALWAYS
> MINOR ERRORS ON MAPS.

Let me also state this clearly: We are not looking for treasure maps where X marks the spot. That kind of map is fiction and isn't what we are seeking. I'm dearly hoping to train my readers to understand what mapping research assets they can expect to find in the United States.

CITY MAPS

I will divide population centers into three groups—village, town, and city—based on increasing size so that this makes sense to people outside the United States as well.

Most cities will have what is known as a city engineer, who is responsible for infrastructure within the city. The name of the department may be different from city to city. It may be called the city manager's office, city planning, urban planning office, or a "manageable growth council" or some such. Just inquire as to who is in charge of the infrastructure, then call them about maps. The city's archive may possess old maps going back to the city's inception. To find where the old maps are, you will need to talk to someone in-the-know at the city engineer's office.

It is quite unlikely that these maps are scanned and available online. You will likely need to research these and see them in person. Getting copies of them may not be possible, but you can bring a high-resolution camera and tripod and snap a picture of them on the ground while they are flat. A good digital camera will capture a phenomenal amount of detail off the map, enough to make the photo a useful resource to you. Don't even think about taking a photo without a tripod. You will likely be given permission to photograph them, but you will not have any control over lighting, so expect low light. A simple tripod will get you plenty of stability. I also recommend you bring four to six heavy (and clean!) lug nuts as map weights to keep scrolled-up maps from trying to re-scroll while photographing them. Just a hint from someone who has been there.

I want to be clear. Captain Hook bullshit treasure maps are not on our list of useful cartographic resources!

Towns and villages may only have old plat maps available at the county courthouse. If the town was bigger back in the day, there may be Sanborn maps available.

For towns and villages, the best resource will likely be USGS historical aerial imagery.

COUNTY MAPS

Most counties in the United States have the responsibility to collect taxes on real estate and to approve new subdivision plats (maps). Both of these responsibilities mean they usually have archives of old maps and plats. The name of the office that has these plats and maps will vary from state to state; your job is to ask around to find the right department in the county government.

STATE MAPS

States have lots of need for maps and mapping analysis. The government needs to know about land use, land change, urbanization speed, disaster preparedness, natural resources, and congressional districts.

Every state has someone in charge of mapping resources, usually the same agency that is in charge of GIS datasets. All you have to do is identify which agency you need and then seek out their map catalog. Almost every state has their mapping assets indexed thoroughly, but only a few have all their maps scanned and available online. So you will need to travel to get access to these maps. Bring a tripod and camera to take good photos in the event they can't make copies.

FEDERAL USGS

The federal government has the same needs as the states, but on a bigger scale. They have put all their mapping needs onto the USGS, so we'll focus there.

The USGS stands for the United States Geological Survey. They are a government agency that creates maps, archives aerial photos, and provides impartial evaluations on the environment and resources in the United States and elsewhere. Their main mission is to provide timely, relevant, and usable map data for other government agencies. Because the USGS was established in 1879, it has a plethora of historical data that is useful to researchers.

Two resources of the USGS that are quite useful to a treasure hunter are:

Historical Topographic Maps - *http://nationalmap.gov/historical/index.html*

USGS historical imagery is the best-kept secret in treasure hunting!

The War Department, the USGS, the US Department of Agriculture, the US Navy, and other agencies have commissioned aerial overflights of the United States since before World War II. Recently, the USGS has begun scanning these images and making them available online at *EarthExplorer.usgs.gov* as TIFF formats.

These images are officially classified as "Aerial Photography, Aerial Photo Single Frame." The good news is these photos are very high quality. The planes flew overflights from 8,000 feet to 35,000 feet, and, as far as I can determine, with excellent results. Lower altitude generally makes for better, higher-resolution imagery. The average imagery overlap is 50 percent, so if one photo doesn't have good focus on your target, the others may.

EarthExplorer can show you the footprints of these photos overlaid on Google Maps so that you can tell how big each photograph is without having to download it. Because smaller footprints correspond to higher quality, it gives you a quick idea of resolution level.

The other nice feature is the abundant metadata built into each photograph, which includes time of day, altitude, image size in megabytes, camera focus length and equipment, total photos taken on the flight, etc. Again, look for low-altitude, small-footprint photos to get the highest resolution.

The bad news is the EarthExplorer interface is clunky and unfriendly. Also, you need to register, which is free (as of March 2012), to be able to download imagery. Another drawback is that the imagery is not oriented with north up. You will have to stare at the photograph and figure out from old roads which way is north. Take care to look at shadows on buildings to help you orient the photo.

A note on resolution and film quality: The photographs from the '40s aren't very high resolution. But by the '60s, the aerial photographs are almost as good as what you get out of commercial satellite imagery, but in black and white. Peruse these images, and you'll understand quickly.

These historical photographs are all initially being scanned as 25 micron (1000 dpi), with some being scanned at high resolution at 14 micron (1800 dpi). You have an option to pay for some 25 micron scanned at high resolution (14 micron). This is their "On Demand" option, and they make it a little difficult, but for only $30 per scan, it is more than reasonable. After all, where else can you get a scanned image of a target that is 50 years old? The good news is if anyone has paid for a high-resolution scan already, you have access to it free.

To guide you through the painful interface over at EarthExplorer.usgs.com, the good folks at the Institute for Mapping Technology put together some practical and short videos on how to use the USGS to extract historical imagery. I highly recommend you watch the videos over at *www.*

LearningGIS.com to quickly master the EarthExplorer inter-face. The instructions at the USGS are terrible.

COMMERCIAL HISTORICAL IMAGERY

Tobin is a company that understood the value of aerial imagery in World War I. It then used surplus war cameras and planes to create a catalog of images in oilfield areas of Texas. The purpose was to then create maps for the oil industry. Consequently, they now have a large historical archive which, unfortunately, isn't digital or online.

The company has now been bought by P2 Energy, and you will have to contact their staff with your imagery needs.

In the case of Texas, we have Tobin. Wherever you live, there may be an equivalent company. It is up to you to discover that company.

NOAA'S US COAST SURVEY HISTORICAL MAPS

The coastline of the United States is important to both shipping and defense. Because of this, over a century ago the government commissioned charts be made of the US coasts. These have now fallen into the hands of the NOAA, and they have been scanned.

These charts show nautical items, but they will also show where cities, towns, and villages are on the coastline. In some cases, they even draw the location of buildings on the beach areas.

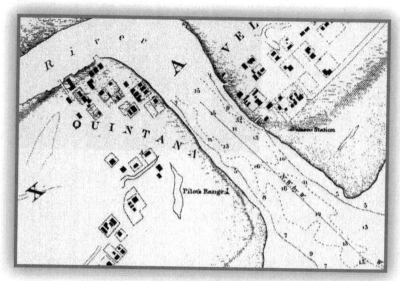

**Here you can see the US Coast Survey maps
show buildings. Quintana, Texas 1856.**

You can find this wonderful Deep Web resource at *http://
historicalcharts.noaa.gov/historicals/search*

These charts typically cover from the 1800s to current times.
There is no guarantee that your local area may be covered, but
if you are on the East Coast, you will have older maps available.

The NOAA archives contain not just the US Coast Survey but
other nautical charts as well, like charts around China, Puerto
Rico, and the Northwest. Some even date back to the 1700s.
These charts are much larger scale and do not have the refine-
ment of small features like buildings.

Copano, Texas, was the main port of entry for European immigrants to Texas. Now a ghost town on private property.

The Confederacy was blockaded during the Civil War, but there was a great deal of activity in blockade running, and impromptu ports were made up some rivers to service this temporary fleet. Coastal Surveys probably won't have them, but you should discover them through other resources.

AERIAL ARCHEOLOGY

Now that you are in the know about the awesome historical aerial imagery at EarthExplorer, it is time to understand it. If you think, "But it is a picture! I get it! You don't need to show me piddly," then you are going off half-cocked. I will explain.

If you are after an old inn from 1900, and the oldest photograph you got from the USGS was 1964 then you will be in a pickle if the building is no longer there. However, collapsed wood buildings in the country are rarely hauled off to a dump or disposed of offsite. They usually are left to cave in and rot. So you have three items to look for:

1. Old foundations and busted-up bricks can still be spotted.

2. Trees next to buildings can be a telltale giveaway. The building rots, but the tree grows and lives decades longer.

3. The building has rotted, but a footprint remains behind as crop marks, soil marks, or frost marks.

Soil Marks – When a building rots, it tends to darken soil. So, if there is very little vegetation at the time the image was taken, it may show square-like blobs of darker earth where the building was. Plowing may smear the shape from square to round over decades of farming. If the ground is rich, black land soil, you might not see much. In which case, you are out of luck.

Discoloration in light contrast is another soil mark. It shows some human use imprint. Perhaps structure.

Soil Marks show some structures used to be here.

Old collapsed buildings tend to darken the soil.

Crop Marks – The building rotted, but it may not be good earth for vegetation. Often there is repressed growth of local vegetation. If you are lucky and it is in a farm field, it becomes much more obvious. Cereal plants like rye and wheat show up much better than other plants, according to Wikipedia.

Frost Marks – For stone buildings that are long gone, the underlying foundation of the walls may still exist. Because these wall foundations are not very porous, water builds up on them in the wet months. During the night, if there is a frost, you can observe frost lines that outline the hidden wall foundations. This is typically seen in the United Kingdom, Ireland, and Europe mainly because of old Roman walls and foundations.

Targets in the New England area should also see them, but in Texas, never, as our winter lasts about a week.

Depressions – If you are lucky and find a photo taken in the early morning or late evening, you may see shadows indicating slight depressions. These can be natural land variations or possibly a terrain subsidence caused by the collapse of a root cellar or soil compression of an outhouse pit. No guarantees, no deposit, no return. You simply have to get on site and figure out the cause of the depression.

GOOGLE EARTH

Google Earth is different from maps.google.com. Google Earth is a software program that ties into multiple vintage WMS imagery servers back at Google. Thus, Google Earth has older imagery available, but it only goes back 10 years at this time.

It can, however, be a quick and effective tool to spot crop marks and soil marks that may be building footprints you need for reference. Do be sure to use Google maps to record the latitude and longitude of the feature. Then you can use most any GPS, plug in that coordinate to the GPS, and then have your GPS guide you to that spot.

> *Most of the time, you can't see a crop mark or soil mark from ground level so be sure to plug it into your GPS before going to the location.*

From the standpoint of a GIS user, Google Earth is nothing but a toy. The real power in mapping is in GIS. Although that may be far more advanced than we can cover in this book, I'll quickly give an overview of GIS and what it means.

GIS

GIS stands for Geographical Information System. It is mapping software—basically a map tied to a database. Any element of the map can be analyzed to show trends in the database on the map.

> *I'll be frank, unless you are a computer whiz, go ahead and bypass this sub-chapter and go to the next. I only expect 10 percent of readers to understand this tool.*

Data for the map is called a "layer." County, state and federal governments have many data layers for the public to use, from landcover, to hydrology, cultural, boundaries, ownership parcels, toxic waste sites, and forest types. Unfortunately, there are no "treasure-is-here" layers.

However, there is a vast array of geospatial data that can be helpful to a treasure hunter, like topography, hydrology, roads, elevation, and ownership parcels. Together these layers will give you the lay of the land and help you figure out where mounted armies would have to ford rivers and who owns these lands now.

Quantum GIS is a free, powerful GIS program that can help you make custom maps of your area of interest.

You can get a full-blown GIS program for free called Quantum GIS (nicknamed QGIS) at Qgis.org. If you want a commercial software program that does the same thing but costs $1,600, then go check out ESRI who will also sell you free datasets for high prices!

Second, there are oodles of datasets out there for QGIS. One big repository is at EarthExplorer.usgs.gov.

There are tutorials on how to extract data from USGS on the quite handy website of LearningGIS.com courtesy of the Institute for Mapping Technology. They also offer online GIS training to crash course you into a functioning GIS user in a matter of a day. I'll stick my neck out and endorse their GIS 101 course as I have taken it. It was a great way to avoid two years of geography and become a power GIS user.

CHAPTER TEN

LIBRARY RESOURCES

The Deep Web has a phenomenal collection of data in it. However, at some point you will need to get yourself into a library for deeper digging. All the Internet did for us, really, was offload some of our library time onto laptop time. You will still need to visit librarians and libraries, and be sure to play nice with the librarians.

Even the smallest library will likely have the ability to do ILL (inter-library loan) requests. You just need to know which book you want and what library has it, and your nice librarian can make the request.

Local libraries often have genealogy sections, so that is a place to hunt down certain people in leads.

**All serious research projects lead to a library.
Embrace them, as you will be good friends.**

If you want to see an example of amazing online research resources, collections, and databases that you can use at a large public library, check out San Francisco's library online, sfpl.org. Unfortunately, you have to be a patron to use these resources.

If you look for "articles and databases" at fpl.org/index. php?pg=2000028601, you will see dozens of resources, several of which are mentioned in this book. Your local library should have some of these resources.

OLD TOPOS

Old topographic maps can be found online at USGS.gov, at the state land mapping office, and sometimes in a large university's map collection.

Usually universities don't have their topographic maps scanned. The USGS and the states often do. So with luck, you'll find the maps you seek online without having to do field trips to map rooms and photograph topos.

If the USGS doesn't have a topo in the year range you are looking for, the state office or a university collection might! Don't be surprised to find gaps in government collections; it happens.

SANBORN MAPS

Insurance. Normally, I can't stand insurance companies, but for once they did something wonderful. The Sanborn Company did an aggressive program a century ago when it mapped out large US cities and drew where all the buildings were located: barns, stables, outhouses, and any other structures. Their plan was to identify all fire risks to structures.

Wikipedia does a much better job describing them:

The Sanborn Maps were originally created for assessing *fire insurance* liability in urbanized areas in the *United States*. The maps include detailed information regarding town and building information in approximately 12,000 U.S. towns and cities from 1867 to 2007.

They are a highly useful resource for historical research, planning, preservation, *genealogical* research, *sociological* studies and research of urban geography.

Mapping for insurance, and specifically fire insurance, purposes had existed for a century prior to the emergence of the Sanborn Company, first beginning in *London* in the late

18th century. In the decades following the end of the *Civil War*, fire insurance mapping grew rapidly, mirroring the flourish of growth in the country, the rebuilding of the South and massive westward expansion. Factors such as the *Homestead Act, railroad* construction, the *Industrial Revolution* and massive *immigration* into the United States all fostered huge population growths, urbanization, and heightened demand for mapping.

The Sanborn Company began making fire insurance maps in 1867 when founded by *Daniel Alfred Sanborn*, a surveyor from *Somerville, Massachusetts*. The Sanborn Map Company created maps for fire insurance assessment in the U.S. and within several decades became the largest and most successful American map company. Sanborn was headquartered in *Pelham, New York*, but had regional offices in *San Francisco, Chicago*, and *Atlanta*. The Sanborn Company sent out legions of surveyors to record the building footprints and relevant details about these buildings in all major urbanized areas regarding their fire liability. It was because of these details and the accuracy of the Sanborn maps, coupled with the Sanborn Company's standardized symbolization and aesthetic appeal that made the Sanborn Company so successful and their maps so widely utilized.

The Sanborn maps themselves are large-scale *lithographed* street plans at a scale of 50 feet to one inch (1:600) on 21 inch by 25 inch sheets of paper. The maps were created in volumes, bound and then updated until the subsequent volume was produced. Larger cities would have multiple volumes. In between volumes, updates (new drawings of new or altered buildings or lots) were created and sent out to be pasted on top of the old maps (referred to as 'slips') to reduce expense and preserve accuracy.

The volumes contain an enormous amount of information. They are organized as follows: a decorative title page, an index of streets and addresses, a 'specials' index with the names of churches, schools, businesses etc., and a master index indicating the entirety of the mapped area and the sheet numbers for each large-scale map (usually depicting four to six blocks) and general information such as population, economy and prevailing wind direction. The maps include outlines of each building and outbuilding, the location of windows and doors, street names, street and sidewalk widths, property boundaries, fire walls, natural features (*rivers, canals,* etc.), railroad corridors, building use (sometimes even particular room uses), house and block number, as well as the composition of building materials including the framing, flooring, and roofing materials, the strength of the local fire department, indications of sprinkler systems, locations of fire hydrants, location of water and gas mains and even the names of most public buildings, churches and companies."[10]

These maps provide the best high-resolution record of American urbanization available with few exceptions.[11]

---

10. Sanborn Maps. Wikipedia, The Free Encyclopedia, The Wikimedia Foundation, Inc., 22 April 2012, Web.
11. Keister, Kim (May/June 1993). "Charts of Change." Historic Preservation 45 (3): 42–49.

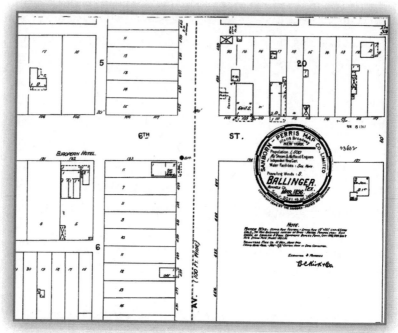

Sanborn maps used a simplistic style as seen here. Note the level of detail of building placement. Can you understand why such maps still hold value? Credit — Sanborn Maps, fair use.

Sanborn maps can usually be accessed via your library, be it your local or state library. This will come from a subscription your library has with the current owner of Sanborn Maps. Alternatively, you can access the catalog of Sanborn maps via the Library of Congress, but only a few of the maps are permitted to be downloaded via the Library of Congress.

COUNTY HISTORY BOOKS

This should be your main starting point for any target class. This is where you find many, many leads. Why? Because county history books provide the finest granularity of events for an area.

County history books are often compiled by passionate retired men and women who've done a huge amount of research for you. The entire book should be considered a secondary source of good authority. It will point you toward the primary sources from which you can glean more information and determine the author's bias.

State history books cover large-scale happenings and events, such as wars and names of battles. The local county history book, however, would supply the name and locations of the exact battles fought, possible maps of these battles, and tidbits of lore surrounding the men who were in these battles. You can then take down notes of these men and the citation of the primary source these accounts are from. Now you have new primary sources to hunt down, with more clues, and a juicy location. From the memoirs, you may find out where the area was for the winter encampment, and, perhaps by checking with old USGS topographic maps, you can locate the exact encampment.

> *Amazingly, being a treasure-hunting researcher does not draw young, buxom, beautiful woman to you at parties. Trust me—I've tried repeatedly for years.*

Of all the secondary sources you will encounter, the local county history book should stay on the top of the list as the most valuable. If you are lucky, you may have more than one for your area. Your job is to learn how many there are, obtain copies—digital or otherwise—and read them. The bad news is most local county history books are highly prized and may have a high cost on them. I recommend talking to a librarian who deals with genealogists about old county history books. Librarians will know most of them, but don't be surprised if you discover a digital copy of a rare county history book that even the librarian doesn't know about. (All hail Archive.org!) After all, they only curate what they have, and if they don't have a copy and have never seen one, then they can't tell you about it.

WHERE TO GET YOUR LOCAL HISTORY BOOKS?

I'll start with the easiest and the free:

Archive.org – An excellent online resource with phenomenal coverage. No guarantees that they will have the book you want, however. Archive.org is covered in depth elsewhere in this book.

Library – Check the local library first, then the local historical society, then the state library. To save yourself multiple trips, librarians have solved the mystery of which library has what by making the excellent tool of WorldCat.

Worldcat and ILL – *www.worldcat.org* – A compendium of library catalogs in one handy place. All you need to do is put in your zip code, tell it the book you are after, and it will tell you the closest library with your book. It will also mention if the book is non-circulating (non-circulating means it can't be checked out) or not. Once you know who has the book, you can go to your local library and put in an ILL request (inter-library loan) for the book if it is a circulating book. You don't even have to travel!

Now for the non-free:

Amazon – Amazon.com is a commercial web book dealer that also has affiliates. Hopefully, you already have heard of these folks. They have a huge selection of books. The affiliates have out-of-print and rare books.

Abe Books – Abebooks.com is a consortium of book dealers who list their stocks collectively on one site—a better selection of rare books, in my humble opinion. Priced about the same as Amazon.

Bookfinder.com – I like to use Bookfinder initially, over Amazon and Abe, as it groups all the books by an author. So instead of having 12 listings of Gone with the Wind, you have just one. Thus, I locate the book quickly. Once I find a listing of the book I'm after, I then switch over to Amazon or Abe to purchase it.

Research Unlimited – *www.research-unlimited.com* – The world's largest treasure book dealer. They have hundreds of treasure books, Civil War reference books and ID guides, Indian history, Old West history, maps, mining, gold panning, pirates, railroads, research books, trail guides, and other books of interest to treasure hunters and for history buffs. They don't have rare books, however. For those who know of Karl Von Mueller, this is the company that morphed out of Examano Press.

Local Used Book Store – This is a long shot. The area you are focusing on may have a bookstore or two. These should have a history section, including local history. What you find in the local history section could be very interesting and provide many new leads. Look for books like A Guide to Old Churches in Walbash Community or Education in Caddo County: 1850-1890 or My Life as a Pioneer: John Doe 1860-1922.

CENSUS

A census is merely a "counting of the people." Ancient Egypt is thought to have started census taking around 3000 BC, and the Ancient Greeks did them as well. The United States is fairly new to the game; we only have 200+ years of doing a census.

In the United States, detailed census records are released 80 years after the census is done. So in 2010-2019, the 1930 census records are now out. The census will tell you who the head of household was, the names of the people living in that house and their occupations (excluding slaves), and sometimes the net worth of the individual. Census questions have changed over time, naturally.

You can access these records online, but the biggest problem is going to be the old style handwriting. Some of the census takers had either overly floral handwriting or abysmal handwriting. However, in treasure hunting, it becomes very important to discover where people were during certain decades.

There are many, many genealogy websites that explain how to look up census records, so I won't cover them here. Just know that you can get to them when needed. Ancestry.com and HeritageQuest are a couple of many commercial, for-fee genealogy websites. For a modest monthly fee, it can make your search-of-census work go much quicker.

Your library, also, usually has a subscription to it that you can use. Just inquire. They likely will have a means so that you can access the library's census record online from your home and not online at their building.

Census Record

You can access some raw census records from archive.org and also from mapserver.lib.virginia.edu, but neither is as user friendly as the tools the library should have.

OLD TAX RECORDS

These are usually held on a county-by-county basis. A call to the courthouse may be all you need to see if the archives are sent up to state level or squirreled away at a COG (County of Governments) facility.

Courthouses hold land transfer records. There is
normally a handy Grantee/Grantor index.

OLD PLATS

First, you may ask, "What is a Plat?" It is merely a map of
ownership boundaries of property. Because the map only deals
with cadastre (ownership boundaries), it is called a plat. Why
didn't they call it an "ownership map"? I have no idea.

Plats are useful as references (albeit they aren't usually to
scale), but they give you an idea of who owned what, where,
and when. Sometimes they include landmarks used by surveyors, just don't count on it.

Be careful of north arrows on any map—it may be true north or magnetic north. The difference can put you off considerably depending on your target. Go to the Wikipedia definition of magnetic declination to understand why.

Plats are usually kept in the county courthouse, and a trip to the courthouse will educate you on the fine points. In every state where I've looked at plats, the process to get them was different, so I don't cover that here.

If you tell the staff you are doing genealogy work, they may even come over and help you. It worked for me!

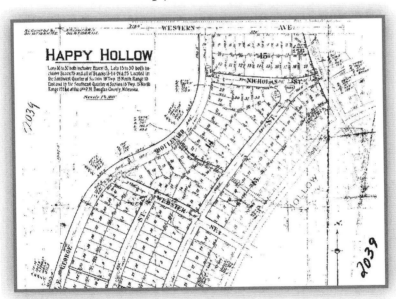

Plats show location of property boundaries.
Photo credit: HistoricOmaha.net

On the whole, the usual use of a plat in treasure research is when you have a name of a person in the county, and you need to find his homestead. So let us say Elmer T. Fudd is a person of interest, and you have no idea where he lives. If you research your plats, you may find an "Elmer Theodorius Fudd" with 50 acres on a plat map, and the years of ownership make it likely you have found the right guy. Now, you have gotten yourself within slingshot range of his house.

OLD YEARBOOKS

Yearbooks document our social lives: who was who, what they did, what they were like, and their friends. To a researcher, they also provide us with a glimpse into the past: photos of people in places—the buildings, the social culture around those buildings, and photos of those buildings in relationship to trees and other buildings. Hint, hint.

If you can't find an aerial photo of the area in the era you are looking for, you may be able to spot the trees that were next to the buildings in a photo. Often the building will be long gone, but the shade trees will survive the building by many decades.

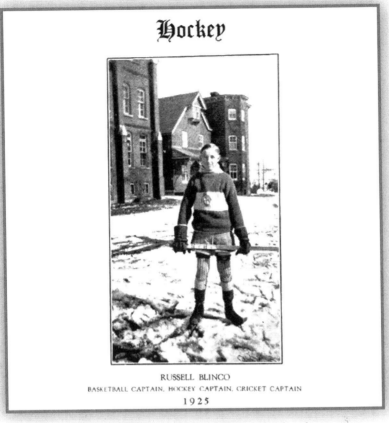

Hockey

RUSSELL BLINCO
BASKETBALL CAPTAIN, HOCKEY CAPTAIN, CRICKET CAPTAIN
1925

Many clues can be derived from yearbooks,
but mostly from the pictures."

Also, the yearbooks provide clues as to where people congregated for parties and festivals. Both locations will aggregate lost coinage.

HISTORICAL SOCIETY LIBRARY

In Texas, most counties have a historical society that collects the cultural knick knacks and artifacts of the region. They also collect all known history books and genealogy books about the area. Because their members are often genealogists and amateur historians, they sometimes author local history books as well. This is a good resource to look into if you have one for your area of interest.

They usually have visiting hours where researchers can come in and peruse the book collection. It won't be as formal as a library, nor will it have the rules. However, they usually have a small budget, so the "viewing room" may be a single desk in a small office with a squeaky chair. Combine that with viewing hours from noon till 1:30 p.m. on Wednesdays only. You get the picture that you need to make room in your schedule to visit and have low expectations of comfort. What you find may boggle your mind and keep you busy for months.

NEWSPAPER COLLECTIONS

Local libraries should have superior newspaper archives on their local newspapers. However, I've been wrong about this a few times as the state library can do a better job if they have grant money. Overall, check your local library first, then the state's.

I've covered more on newspaper archives elsewhere in this book.

CHAPTER ELEVEN

STATE LIBRARY

The state library should have several collections. It also is likely to be the state archive as well, or it might work in conjunction with it. There are several collections that should be of interest to researchers, but what they are called and which one is appropriate will depend on what you seek and what they chose to call it.

To illustrate an example of resources, I'll cover the state library where I live, which is Texas. I looked up the Texas state library, which has the official name of "Texas State Library and Archives Commission." So right there, we know that the state archives will be associated with it or folded into it.

For resources it lists:

- **State Archives and Manuscripts** – Everything from Texas Rangers paymaster slips to after-action reports of the companies in the Civil War

- **State Law Library** – You got it, just law collections

- **Texas Commission on Environmental Quality** – Environmental studies, etc.

- **Genealogy section** – The usual array of genealogy resources: death indexes, birth records, specialty gene-alogy books, etc.

- **Texas Heritage Online** – A digitized and searchable archive of special collections covering history and culture headed by various museums, historical soci-eties, and other institutions; mainly what I found was scanned newspapers from major cities going back to the Civil War era.

GENEALOGY

Juicy stories about a man long dead require lots of research and vetting. You can't just believe nor can you blankly dismiss. Find out what you can about the person, his relatives, his home and society, what he owned and where he lived. Then you can begin to gauge what kind of man he was, whether it makes sense to label him as a miser, a pauper, a rich man, or an average bloke who boasted. You may even discover long-dead relatives who are far more interesting targets for field work and research.

My top focus when I research a target is to determine the cause of death. When the grim reaper takes a soul swiftly and unexpectedly, there is a rational cause to believe a cache was left behind. Then I look for spouses and children and use the scorecard method to rank that lead.

There are several good guides on how to do genealogy studies. I'd recommend you start at *www.ancestry.com* to learn the basics.

I won't explain the nuances of genealogy here. However, you will likely begin at census records, then look into the death index, then go to a courthouse and look at the grantee/grantor index to find properties they owned.

There are many types of records that will be useful; take a look at *www.researchguides.net* to get an understanding of the myriad of records you can pull up. Also understand that 95 percent of the records you will check may pull up a blank; that is just how good research goes. No one said it was easy. But if you skip a few steps, you can miss critical hits that can save you weeks.

Do remember that genealogists are a sharing and trusting bunch. They have several means to tie in each others' genealogy work. Again, Ancestry.com, HeritageQuest, or ResearchGuides.net will aid you there.

PLAT MAPS

Some state archives may have some older, historically significant plats. However, few will have large collections. Plats are mainly useful on a county level, and that is where you will most likely find them. Do take the effort to check the state archive when you can do so easily.

HISTORIC PHOTOS

Photographs are a crapshoot. The average archive may have them organized rationally, or on some screwy system. You will have to use your instincts and intuition to pick the logical categories to peruse looking for a lead.

Mainly, you want photos that aid you in locating the exact location of vetted leads or photographs that spark up a new lead. For instance, if you wanted to find an old lake beach where people swam in the '30s, you'd try to locate the appropriate categories that may show that beach, or a photograph of winners of some swim contest at the beach. But while hunting for your mystery beach, you may find a photograph that shows a different beach you've never heard of nearby and Bingo! You have a new lead!

Trust your instincts. I sense the Force is strong in you by now.

SPECIALTY COLLECTIONS

There are many different types of special collections. At the University of Texas in Austin, they have a special collection of Spanish history books. These are non-circulating and have to be visited to be accessed.

Often famous people will donate their personal papers to a college or university, and these papers wind up in a special collection. For example, Frank Dobie's (who wrote Legends of Texas: Lost Mines and Buried Treasure) collection was donated to the University of Texas.

These collections can be astoundingly useful if they overlap on your target research. My biggest successful treasure jackpot was due to the personal collection of a researcher who donated his papers to a school in North Texas. I browsed the special collections and saw his name and knew that I would need to peruse his file. Lo and behold, he had done field trips to my target location in the 1930s and 1940s and wrote up his findings. With that information and a bit of genealogy, I found my target area within 10 man hours of work. Four days later I found my target and was thrilled for months!

If you are researching a person of interest who could have amassed a collection of papers that may have been donated then do a quick check—the local colleges first, then the logical college that would have been the rational choice to receive the collection. In all cases, the university will have a web listing of the special collections available. Rarely will the collection itself be accessible online.

> *Research projects can start online, but few will complete without a visit to a library.*

NEWSPAPER COLLECTION

Newspapers used to have a "newspaper morgue" where a copy of each newspaper they issued was stored. Consolidations in the industry may have lost some of those morgues, but the digital age caught up with many of them.

The older collections were copied over to microfiche, and you will have to view them the hard way, one page at a time. Some states have digitized some periodicals and newspapers. So go back to the previous discussion on newspaper archives for online resources.

CHAPTER TWELVE

ODDBALL RESOURCES

Think outside the box. What other events happened near your topic of interest? Would those agencies or event managers have records?

Looking for a house in 1932? Was there an oil well within two miles of it? Why not check the filings with the state oil and gas commission? They often included a plat. You just might spot the house on the lease plat.

Did a water or oil pipeline run by the area in the 1940s? Why not hunt down the planning maps, or check to see if there was a line-of-construction overflight made just for that pipeline which might have photos of your target?

Did the CCC build something a few miles away in the 1920s? Why not check their archives to see if they drew maps or took aerials over a wider area?

Was your target area ever involved in a real estate lawsuit? These occurred in the 1800s as well. Mankind hasn't changed after all. Maybe there are maps filed in the courthouse documents. A check at the courthouse clerk's office is a long shot but could be worth it. See if you can check the filings index online, first.

Hunting a cache in a sudden-demise case? Don't forget to pull his will. You may find enlightening items there that could shut the lead down. Check.

CHAPTER THIRTEEN

OLD PEOPLE

I have to put our esteemed elderly in here as a resource. They are the living history of the area. I always encourage researchers to talk to them. Better yet, go visit retirement, rest homes, and old folks' homes as they have lots of free time. If you can steer the conversion, you will get plenty of new leads along with verification of your past research. In my experience, you will have to carefully vet their stories as our elderly often get the "who, when, and where" a bit muddled up sometimes.

Our elders are a wealth of information. Ask!
Photo credit: Mauricio Fotografia

Bear in mind that when in the field, you should enjoy yourself and your research. So open up to these old timers and truly enjoy the experience as they chat down memory lane. They often are hard up for someone to talk with, and you are doing a good deed while doing research. Also, don't be shy about telling them you are doing research on local history. It is a true statement, and you will also make them feel more important, which helps to lubricate the social gears.

... open up to these old timers and truly enjoy the chat...

You will hear stories of very interesting incidents and quirky events. Keep your ears focused and a pad and pen in your hand.

I'd recommend asking about:

- moonshiners and Prohibition

- misers

- robberies

- murders

- revival meetings

- big picnic areas

- swimming holes

- local merchants who used trade tokens

- informal racetracks or gambling houses

- scandalous, old bordello buildings

- and lastly, stories of missing money, but be careful how you approach this. If you ask about treasure hunting, you might get an earful of funny tales.

This interviewing process can last from a few minutes to an hour. It would be best to develop a relationship over time, perhaps drop in on each time you are nearby. Don't forget to bring some sweets as old folks in rest homes usually don't have access to candy. It's worth more than gold to them, and it is good for the soul to do random acts of kindness.

You will need to corroborate and vet the stories you hear. We are all fallible and likely to repeat tales that we've not vetted. It is a flaw of the human condition.

I'd also recommend bringing whatever map you have of the area, be it an old topographic map, an old atlas, or something you've printed out. It can serve as a great guide for jogging their memories and getting a higher quality account from them.

CHAPTER FOURTEEN

RESEARCH WORKFLOW

START WITH THE END IN MIND— PICK YOUR TARGET CLASS

I have two primary classes I research: the first is a specialty "other" class and the other is the cache class focusing on those who met a sudden demise in their 30s or 40s. Also, I'll search for coin-hunting grounds as a backup plan because cache hunting can run long dry spells, and I need to keep myself motivated by finding something. I'm sure you can relate.

So where do I go for leads? The first place I start is the local county history book.

> *On Expectations - You should strive for a range somewhere near a 5:1 to 2:1 ratio of hours doing research to hours in the field. It depends on the size of the project.*

COUNTY HISTORY BOOK

There are usually several county history books for any given county. You should have a copy of the latest one on your shelf. The others must be researched online to find, and hopefully Archive.org has a copy.

My plan is just to read the book and pay attention to places of interest like schools, fairgrounds, races, general stores, and churches. I take notes on the item and on what page it's described so that I can cross-reference these leads later. I also am watching out for nefarious items such as murders, skirmishes, and battles. Sudden death always carries the potential for caches, so I mark these down in my notes, and what I know about them.

I do take care to read the entire book. I pay attention to all references of sources and jot them down as well. Books mentioned, papers, collections, and both primary and secondary sources are all welcome.

ARCHIVE.ORG

Next I'll go to archive.org and look for other county books mentioned and any of the other books mentioned. Then I search for other books that may be relevant to the county or area involved. Quite often weird and wonderful books will pop up such as History of Rural Schools in XXXX.

Archive.org always has the potential to uncover completely unknown sources for you.

CENSUS

For my "sudden demise" cache targets of interest, I'll try to find the person on the census and see if he had a wife or kids. I'll review his land holdings to try to establish his level of wealth, while also taking into account his number of kids.

The idea here is to figure out if the spouse likely knew where he hid the money.

LIBRARY

No credible research project can be done only online. At some point, sources are identified, and they can't be found online due to rarity or copyright restrictions, so I'll likely make a trip to the library and complete an ILL request. I never forget to smile at my librarians; they are awesome.

GOOGLE EARTH OR GOOGLE MAPS

If I think I kind of know where the target is, I'll check on it with Google Maps or Google Earth. It gives me a good idea of the region, and I can then start pulling historical imagery from USGS which uses Google Maps as a base map.

Bear in mind, EarthExplorer.usgs.gov will often have better aerial photos of an area in a rural setting, and a more recent image as well. Frankly, Google can't touch USGS for quality.

USGS HISTORIC IMAGERY

The first thing I do is head over to EarthExplorer.usgs.gov. Then I set the red box over my AOI (area of interest) with four corners. Then I set the date range to be (say) 1920-1970 to try to find any imagery available. Of course I choose the data set of "single frame photos," which are the historical scans.

EarthExplorer usually offers up a dozen images or so. Immediately, I'll blink (turn on and off) the footprint button on each image to get an idea of what it covers relative to my red box AOI. For the one that covers it best, I check out the meta data to see the altitude of the flight and take note of it. Then I download the image, rotate it to have north as up, and see what I can see.

I repeat the above step with other images that covered my AOI, and usually one of them stands out as highest quality with good resolution.

These images can be large, between 50 MB and 120 MB. A fast Internet connection is quite helpful.

The best-kept secret resource for metal detecting is the USGS EarthExplorer. Learn it, use it, love it.

USGS TOPO MAPS

On the USGS website, I find their historical topographic map section and search for the nearest town to my AOI. Hopefully, USGS will have multi-year selections returned to me as options. I choose the year that is closest to my event and download it.

It usually appears with north up, so I just have to figure out where my AOI is relative to the roads shown. This is a big time drain sometimes, figuring out where I am relative to current photos.

FIELD VISIT – RECON

By now, I should have a good idea of where the old buildings were in my AOI. I just need to get ground truth. So I pick a weekend, throw in my nice hat, and scoot off to the AOI.

When I arrive, I ask questions of anyone who is outside, trying to find the landowners of my AOI and any local historians. Then I'll hunt down the landowners and use map-out protocol to ask permission.

FIELD – EXPLOITATION

Next, I have a blast detecting at a virgin site!

CHAPTER FIFTEEN

HOW TO DO PROPER RECONNAISSANCE

HOW TO DO PROPER RECONNAISSANCE

Good research eventually leads to a need to establish ground truth aka reconnaissance, i.e. you have photos of the target area, but what is really there now?

Good reconnaissance is about assessment of the lay of the land, the landowners, the terrain, the obstacles to searching, the local human resources, the legal challenges, and the overall "Do-ability" of the hunt.

If I only had four hours with boots on the ground, I would focus on:

- **Houses nearby** – Is the target landowner living in one of them?

- **Terrain** – Start taking photographs at the highest resolution that your camera can handle. Use a monopole to keep the camera steady. Tripods draw too much attention; monopoles are more discrete and are acceptable gear for birders and nature lovers.

- **Talk to anyone outside** – Say that you are doing research (you are) and ask if there is a local historian or old timer who knows local history. While you have them talking, ask where your target landowner lives and what they can tell you about the owner.

- **Approach a nearby house** – If no one is out. Ask the same questions. Be sure to use the map-out protocol to be disarming. (Map-out protocol is covered later.)

- **Seek the historian or old timer** – They know more than you. Seek and inquire.

When you get to a new location, just ask
someone. They usually will point you to the local
historian. Photo credit: John Steadman.

After your recon or hunt is over, you should write up a single paragraph summary of your findings. This will be very helpful to you in the future.

LOCAL LIBRARIAN KNOWS ALL

The local librarian is a librarian because they love knowledge and information. They aren't civil servants because it was the only job they could get. Librarians are unheralded heroes to researchers; they can provide insights that you weren't expecting, lead you to resources you've never heard of, and find the same things you can find—but faster. Be nice and treat them well.

"Librarians are the secret masters of the universe. They control information. Never piss one off." —Spider Robinson, "The Callahan Touch" Photo credit: Rochelle Hartman.

Currently, there is a mandate that libraries must have publicly available Internet. This has resulted in librarians being delegated the responsibility of babysitting the public. Many librarians I've spoken with are quite resentful of this duty, and therefore will be quite enthusiastic about a true research project that gives them a challenge.

I'd encourage you to be honest about your topic and tell them you are doing research for a pet project. Don't hide behind a lie as human nature can sometimes detect something is wrong, and you will lose their enthusiasm to help you. On the flip side, don't say "I'm looking for treasure." Say perhaps, "I want to find the house location of John P. Moorganhein in 1823."

ASKING PERMISSION – THE MAP-OUT PROTOCOL

Asking permission to get on someone's land and hunt coins with a metal detector was an insurmountable challenge to me when I first started out. If there are others who are like that, I want to quickly delve into this off-topic and give some quick tips to make your life easier.

I was 16—and shy—when I got my first metal detector. Mr. Garrett didn't give any kind of advice for a shy detectorist in his books, so I never had the courage to knock on doors for permission to explore juicy-looking areas. Now that I know the ropes, I wish I could tell the 16-year-old me how to do it. At least I can tell you . . .

I call it the map-out protocol. It has four components to it:

1. Dress above average for the area—no dirty nails and stained shirt. In Texas, nice boots, new blue jeans, and a button-up shirt are fine. I'd opt for a cool hat, too.

2. Have a map (of the local area) out in your hands and read it when approaching the door as well as after you ring the doorbell. Dogs in the house may have alerted the owners to you, so you want to be seen reading the map.

3. Ring the doorbell, STEP BACK several paces, focus on your map, and turn so that your side is to the door.

4. When they answer the door, you turn to them, smiling, and simply say, "I don't THINK I'm lost, BUT . . ." and ask a couple of questions about the area you are in and who owns what. Stress the words I've capitalized. If you've talked to a neighbor, mention that.

Why this works is a really fascinating piece of sociology:

1. You have a map out, so they know you aren't selling anything or with the government. Thus, they don't have their highest guard up. Also, people judge you within seconds of meeting, and here you are disarming and smiling, +2 for your side.

2. You look lost, and there is something in our cultural identity to help the lost guy. So suddenly, a stranger goes from being defensive at his front door to WANTING to help you—a bizarre twist in psychol-

ogy. I'm sure there is a PhD thesis waiting for a grad student right there.

e.   If you mentioned you talked to a neighbor, you now have the power of social proof. As in, "If the neighbor talked to him, he must be OK."

This works for me 90 percent of the time. It fails the other 10 percent because they were pressed for time to pick up a spouse, in the middle of a meal, or some other random factor that wasn't about me and was beyond my control.

So at this point, the person on their front porch is trying to help you. You've asked a few questions about the area, the land-owners, the owners of the target property, and the history.

If you've confirmed that you are speaking to the landowner, the next thing to do is to bring up a little about your research. Here is where you need to understand what you think the owner will react favorably to. You mention that you want to write up some local history and that you'd like to have the fun of locating the old buildings using your metal detector. Then you simply pop the question: "Is it okay if I walk your land and use my metal detector to try to locate the buildings?" And that is when the owner will give you the nod. For coinshooting, it is bad form to ask for written permission to hunt. You will just triple your chances that he will say no. However, if he says yes to a verbal request, you can always later ask, "Hey, I will be coming back in the next few days. Is there someone who watches your land, and would it be a good idea to have a note from you that it is okay?" It is nice to have this, and I've done it many a time. The properties I was on were 160 to 640 acres, so it made sense to both of us.

Your main goal is to look mildly lost. Social mores will aid you with the rest.

But ask them to sign a salvage agreement? Nooooo! Bad, bad idea. That would raise questions. If it ever goes to court, you've already screwed up badly, and that document won't help you much. Discretion is key—and keep smiling.

Do be a good boy (or girl) and get the owner's phone number and your card. Make sure your card is a boring I'm-just-an-office-worker kind of card. If you were silly enough to have an I'm-an-awesome-treasure-hunter card, then you just screwed yourself. It has served me well to call the owner before I come out about local conditions. I achieve three things: I get a status report, a briefing on local gossip, and I renew the relationship with the owner.

CHAPTER SIXTEEN

TREASURE SENSE AND COMMON SENSE

The year is 1936. You and your wife don't trust banks and want to hide your next season's crop money from thieves. Where do you hide it?

1915, Mexico. Pancho Villa's thugs are raiding local hamlets. They've been seen 50 miles south. Your workers are nervous, and you don't trust them. Where do you hide your plate silver heirlooms?

1944, Germany. The Americans are pushing closer to your monastery and are known looters (which was true). Where would you hide the holy silver and gold relics before you all leave your monastery for safer grounds?

1877, Turkey. The Russian army has laid siege to the town, garrisoning your cavalry company and 200 troops. They will likely break through in under two weeks. Your commanding officer issues orders to hide the payroll funds to avoid it falling into Russian coffers. Where and how will it be hidden?

In all four cases, I want you to put yourself into his shoes—feel his stress, understand the possible loss, comprehend the situation he is in. Then take note of the factors he has to weigh, like witnesses who may see a payroll burial, or nosy neighbors who could do the math and notice that three days after you sold your harvest there is freshly dug earth by the apple tree.

> ## *Feel his stress, understand the possible loss, comprehend the situation he is in.*

Think about what he has to work with and how much time and the number of helpers he has. What is the hiding period expected to be? 10 days, 10 months, 10 years? Does he have a squad of men, a week, and 10 shovels? Two hours and constant gunfire from snipers? Maybe they just dumped it in the well or in the latrine. Are there multiple targets? Did the soldiers themselves bury personal caches with hopes of recovering them later like the Roman army did?

In these four examples, I took care to list them in increasing order of witnesses and resources.

THE FARMER

In the case of a farmer trying to hide his harvest money for nine months, he just needs a safe place nearby.

I'd want to put it within eyesight of where I'd be most of the time. I'd be cautious not to let neighbors see me digging or retrieving. My big concern would be if I'd lose it by forgetting where I buried it. As a precaution I'd be sure to tell my wife where it is, just in case.

I'd also be concerned about fresh dug sod alerting busy bodies that I've buried something. Fence posts would serve dual purposes for me: first, working with fencing would be normal farm activity that wouldn't interest the neighbors; and second, I can spot where it is fairly quickly. However, a better place would be in my root cellar or basement if I had loose bricks or a bare earth floor.

A single man will likely dig a hole no deeper than what his arm can reach. Karl von Mueller pointed this out in one of his books. From field experience, I am now convinced he is right.

THE MEXICAN ESTATE OWNER

Lawlessness and banditry force people to be careful.

I'd be concerned the house would be burned down, so I'd want to bury the silver plate in the garden, in an estate crypt, or another area of taboo that bandits or local kids wouldn't enter. But my workers are watching me as well, and I don't trust their sympathies. Some may report to the other side.

Most likely the core of the family will work together to hide it quickly at night when the workers aren't around—maybe on Sunday when the workers are at mass. But they don't have much time, so they can't get fancy—no complicated signs and symbols on trees requiring complex surveying equipment to find. At most, a nail is driven into a tree, a string and bob hung below, and a hole dug. The hole might be two to six feet deep depending on the urgency and time. When they're done, a large rock will be moved to hide the newly dug soil. They might even put the dirt on a blanket before putting it back over the hole, to minimize the fresh-dug-hole look.

> *But they don't have much time, so there's no time to get fancy—no complicated signs and symbols on trees requiring complex surveying equipment to find.*

If my house had masonry, it would be safer from prying eyes if it were interred behind stone. Basements would be a good spot as well, not to mention beehives where no one but the most thorough would search.

I'd also consider throwing valuables in bags down the well. They can be recovered later in a few weeks.

Firsthand accounts from primary sources during the American Civil War spoke of plantation owners burying goods well behind buildings in the tree line. The accounts also spoke of the Union army soldiers being wise enough to use their reloading ram rods for their muskets as probes to look for silver plate hastily buried in gardens.

THE MONASTERY

Holy relics and golden accouterments are what the locals know you have and thus the Allies will know you have. They need to be hidden, and within the next seven days.

You have more time, lots of resources, and a cadre of men who can be trusted. Where to hide it? If there is a well on sight and a well keeper who knows his well-walls, I'd put it behind a well-wall. I would, of course, leave some golden-leafed goodies as decoys to let the Allies think they pillaged the place.

Throwing relics down the well is not an option. Packing objects up and moving them with wandering monks is not an option, either. Most likely, the monks will choose a burial of some sort, a deep hole (maybe 6–10 feet) is possible, given the time and the manpower. A good deal of thought will be given to covering up the traces of the hole.

The team assigned to bury the gold artifacts needs to be limited to just the monks needed. There is always the possibility of capture and torture.

This game has been played out many times between roving looters and the church, most notably during King Henry VIII's church reformation in England when the king seized church gold, silver, land, and other assets. Much church gold was hidden when word got to the monasteries first.

A good read about the treasure found from the Reformation is documented in Edward Fletcher's Buried British Treasure Hoards.

THE BESIEGED OTTOMANS

Two hundred men encamped in a town under siege by 3,000 pissed-off Russians. Damn, that has to suck.

The commanding officer of the troops knows they will lose and have to surrender. He makes the decision to save lives, but first, he wants to spike the cannons, render the powder useless, destroy or cache small arms, and definitely hide the payroll.

If he lives, he may have ideas about coming back and recovering the payroll for himself. This is the Ottoman culture, after all. But first, he has to bury it in a way that it stays hidden.

I'd assume there will be a good chance the fort structures will be destroyed or burned to the ground, so a hiding spot in a building is out of the question.

Treasure sense is about deeply understanding the pressing problems of the treasure hider.

Burying it makes sense. With a squad of 14 men digging for two days, a 10-15-foot hole could be dug. A landmark would be needed to triangulate it, or it could be near a corner of a building. Witnesses would be the biggest problem. I would have multiple teams digging other holes as "defensive trenches" and only a trusted team of officers digging the deep hole where the payroll would go.

If there were casualties, I would have the payroll buried first then a proper burial of the dead over them. Most cultures have a taboo about disturbing the interred.

I'd expect the Russians to come in, tear the place apart looking for arms, powder, and money. The deeper that hole, the more likely they will give up if they dig in the trenches. Only a spy could spoil the location.

IN CONCLUSION

Note that the complexity of the interment of the valuables increased with the number of witnesses and men available. Single men dug shallow holes, groups of men can go deeper, and for a logical reason. To extrapolate further, governments can and have buried targets at great depth, albeit these targets tend to be defense-industry related.

Small caches with no witnesses are not interred with extraordinary complexity.

Put yourself in the other man's shoes when cache hunting; it will give you better treasure sense.

If you ever learn anything from this book, remember to avoid being besieged by the Russians. It never ends well.

CHAPTER SEVENTEEN

HUNT LOCALLY, RESEARCH LOCALLY

Do not be deluded into thinking that you need to travel hundreds of miles to find good leads on caches, treasures, or ultra sweet coin-hunting grounds. That is just plain bullshit.

Good leads are nearby. Garrett once told me that, and 20 years later I know it to be the truth.

GO FOR DEPTH OF KNOWLEDGE

A phenomenal number of leads will pop up from your local county history book, and there will be more in the archives at the local historical society.

The more you research your initial targets, the more leads you will find on interesting side targets, some of which may be potentially large caches.

Travel costs; time costs; hotel, gas, vehicle and logistical costs can add up in a hurry when you start going farther than an hour from home. I know this personally as I have hunted six hours away and even taken expeditions to South America and Africa.

Stay in your own backyard and learn the history well. It is your advantage over the next guy. Your ability to quickly go into the field every weekend is a major advantage and should be exploited.

If you don't have a competitive advantage – don't compete.

CACHE HUNTING IS SUSTAINABLE

Old West treasures, Prohibition caches, pirate loot—all of those treasures are fixed in number. They were planted, some were found, and new ones cannot be replanted. In other words, it is a dwindling target population.

Caches, however, are still being put down by farmers, businessmen, politicians, and drug dealers. Thus, caches are being renewed every year as there are a statistical number of caches that are never recovered by their owners.

I propose to the newcomer who wants to be a treasure hunter that cache hunting is the way to start. It permits the hunter to find small, enjoyable coinage and artifacts while keeping the door open for a nice, solid payday.

Dr. George MacDonald postulated that there are three reasons for hoarding money in the ground: profit, safety, and fear.[12]

Around the time of Caesar, caches were a known means of securing your wealth, especially in times of conflict. Chronicled here by Appian almost 2,000 years ago is a remarkable insight into the practice.

Thus was Rhodes captured; and Cassius took his seat on the tribunal and planted a spear by the side of it to indicate that he had taken the city by the spear. Laying strict commands upon his soldiers to remain quiet, and threatening with death any who should resort to violence or plunder, he summoned by name about fifty citizens, and when they were brought, put them to death. Others, who were not found, numbering about twenty-five, he ordered to be banished. All the money that was found, either gold or silver, in the temples and the public treasury, he seized, and he ordered private citizens who had any to bring it to him on a day named, proclaiming death to those who should conceal it, together with a reward of one-tenth to informers and freedom in addition to in the case of slaves. At first many concealed what they had, hoping that in the end the threat would not be carried out, but when they saw the rewards paid and those who had been informed against punished, they became alarmed, and having procured the appointment of another day, some of them dug their money out of the ground, others drew it out of wells, and others brought it from tombs, in much larger amounts than the former collections.[13]

---

12. Dr. George MacDonald, read before the Royal Philosophical Society of Glasgow in 1903 on coin hoards.

13. Roman History, Appian, BC, IV, 73.

Rhodes today. War drives money underground
in all eras. Photo credit: James Bird

Some interesting facts pop out here about burying in the ground, under water in their wells, and in tombs. It appears that man hasn't changed much. Note how these Rhodites chose to use a human taboo of not bothering the dead as a means of securing wealth against invaders.

ONE DIRTY SECRET OF TREASURE HUNTING

You may have already surmised this, but let us come clean on it. Overall, more money is spent on treasure hunting than the value of treasure recovered. That has been the rule for centuries. It wasn't until the advent of the metal detector that the rate of loss has dropped. Notice I didn't say stopped, just dropped.

Treasure hunters rarely find treasure. Kids and farmers find it as a random act of happenstance. Most hoards and minor caches found over the centuries were primarily discovered by accident. This is well documented in Great Britain.[14]

There are folks who love coinshooting, but if they sit down and do the math, they will realize they don't make enough to pay for gas to get to their location. Even worse, if successful coin-shooters factor in time, they aren't going to make minimum wage most days.

Hopeless? No, because there is the 5 percent club.

THE 5 PERCENT CLUB

Without a study backing me, I'm going to estimate that 95 percent of treasure hunters are truly just outdoor hobbyists who, when objectively evaluated, aren't making minimum wage. However, that last 5 percent are making good money for their time and expenses involved. Learning good research methods will help you become part of the 5 percent.

That 5 percent is smart with their time, brutal with pruning their leads, and fluid with their research. You will find they quickly attack a project or swiftly abandon a lead. When they score a cache, it wasn't after some 15-year research project, but after 12 hours of research done over six weeks. We must be fair and add into that average the 15 dud leads pruned and the six other projects that they pursued and didn't score on. Let us assume 80 hours of research time for all the good and bad leads and projects examined to recover one cache plus 20 hours of drive time and field time for a total of 100 hours. Let

---

14. Beard, Charles Relly (1933), The Romance of Treasure Trove, London: Sampson Low & Co, OCLC 9567664 note – This is a damn fine book for your collection.

us assume a cache value of $6,000, and the math ($6000/100 hours) leaves us with a reasonable $60 per hour compensation.

The 5 percent move swiftly to a go/no-go decision, then act on it. What they don't do is go search an old homestead just because it is an old homestead. They search a homestead because the rancher who lived there died in a gunfight. The 5 percent hunter is gambling on a high-probability statistic of a cache being nearby. They don't waste time on low-probability target research.

Recognize which group you are in—the 95 percent or 5 percent. Make the effort to become a better hunter and a wiser manager of your time, and you may evolve to the 5 percent club.

WHAT IS YOUR TIME WORTH?

There are hobbies and there are hobbies. Some are financially expensive, and some are time expensive. Dangerous ones are both.

I'm hoping you know by now that your time is worth something. If you are really savvy, then you've already sat down, done the math, and come up with a fairly good number of what one hour of your free time is worth in terms of cash per hour. That is a very good number to know. If you don't know yet, set down this book and give that deep thought and come back to me with an answer. It will come in handy when you think through the research in the rest of this book. In fact, it will come in handy for the rest of your life.

Here, the research process is laid out to maximize the results per research hour. Your time is valuable; don't waste it on bad leads and poor research. Value your time.

You can always make money back, but you can never regain lost time.
- AN OLD ENTREPRENEUR'S ADAGE.

Spend your time wisely. I did warn you this was going to be today's mantra, didn't I?

CHAPTER EIGHTEEN

WHEN TO STOP

Sometimes, you brick it and can't make any more headway in your research on a target. You may get a name, but you can't find anything else on him. Or you get an oblique reference to a lead that is in a county, but no more information on what city or even region in the county. When you have made all reasonable searches, including tax records and land ownership records, update the file with what you do know and put it on hold. A few months or years later, another nugget might show up that may break open the case.

You need to know when to kill a project and when to just pause it.

If you have several primary sources that point to a poor man with no resources, but you have rumors of a large cache, that probably is just a rumor, with no fact. Can it and move your precious time to the next project.

If, instead, you have verified a moonshiner in the area but are stuck on where he lived, then you can pause the project until you find another source on another day that casts light on it.

EMOTIONAL DETACHMENT

Emotions will be the most expensive part of your research if you aren't careful. Some people—and I'm talking about you—can get emotionally attached to a project and refuse to accept the bad-looking evidence of their properly done research. So they tell themselves, "There has to be a cache here!" They will think this after their research tells them the guy was a pauper, sold apples on street corners, survived off of welfare, and lived in a cardboard box under the bridge.

Part of the problem here is that we don't like to be wrong. It is a classic problem in stock market investing with lots of research to back it up. A guy buys 100 shares of stock at $100 a share after researching the stock with evidence that indicates the stock is worth $120 per share.

But six months later the stock trades at $80 per share, so he researches the stock again and finds that it should be worth $50 per share. A rational investor sells immediately at $80 per share and walks away from the loss because he can sell it at a premium over what it is worth. But because human nature hates to be wrong, the average investor thinks, "No, I'll just wait and sell it when it eventually hits above $100 many years from now." Does this sound familiar to anyone?

In this case, your time is what you invested in project research. When you evaluate your target and conclude you have a dud, you need to cut your losses and stop. Sometimes that can be very hard. But do it. Your time is valuable—don't waste more on a bum project. Avoid throwing good time after bad.

CHAPTER NINETEEN

RECORD KEEPING

FIELD USABILITY OF RESEARCH

Every good treasure hunt will take you out to the field. You really, really need to be prepared with all your data, which means your file on this target should be printed out for field use.

I don't care that you have your data all on .doc files, zotero, and backed up in the cloud. It does you no good, 15 miles into the desert, when you have no power let alone no Internet!

You will find features out in the field that make you think, "Ah ha!" as you recall some weird tidbit you read in a primary, first-hand account. You will want to re-read that because you understand it now that you are in the field.

Thus, I fully encourage you to do this old school and print out all your files and carry them around with you in a portable file carry. Tablets and iPads are not up to the challenge, yet.

CHAPTER TWENTY

EXAMPLE WORKFLOWS

In the evolution of every chess player, there comes a time when the player has to read specific books in order to evolve. In chess, these books are well known, and one of them is Logical Chess Move by Move, Every Move Explained by I. Chernev. This is a book that will be read early as it helps form the player's thought processes. There is great value in looking over someone's shoulder and seeing how they make their decisions.

In the didactic spirit of looking-over-the-shoulder, I will do the same for my researching decisions.

Example 1 – Downs Field

For the coinshooters, I'll start with a coin-hunting target. I'm looking for an old ball field. I choose a ball field at random.

So I pull up USGS historical topo maps first, for my area. Why did I choose to go to the USGS first? Simple. The field will be a large feature on a map and should be easily identifiable. If I were looking for a carnival grounds, this wouldn't work because the carnival could have set up on any large, empty lot on the edge of town and wouldn't be labeled. But a ball field is labeled, as you can see on the topo.

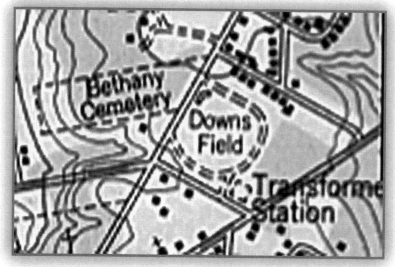

Photo credit: USGS

The one that makes the most sense is a 1954 topo map as I want to find silver not clad. I also want to find one that is no longer a ball field and is back to being a vacant lot so that I won't have competition. Plus it would increase my chances of being the first hunter there.

Well, next I find the same location on Google Maps and get a rude surprise. Something has been built on the ball field— an elementary school. From the topo, I suspect the bleachers would be on the north side, so there may be a little detecting that could be done there, but I'd recommend a small coil.

Image credit: Google Maps and GeoEye

I'd freeze any further research on this, and I'd rack this up as a lukewarm success for research.

Estimated research time spent: 30 minutes

Example 2 – Austin Sanatorium

Sanatoriums are places where they sequestered tuberculosis patients to help them improve. In medical hindsight, the biggest health gain was removing infected vectors from the population.

But I figured it would be a good place to find lost coins and interesting things patients may have dropped.

I chose this target because I spotted it on the 1954 topo while looking for ball fields. So a chance glance gave me this lead. Because it was out at the edge of town in the '50s, I was hoping it was still undivided land.

When I looked at the Google Map imagery, I was amazed to find not only the land intact, but the buildings still standing, and no further construction had occurred on it. I wondered about that. Could it still be a sanatorium? But good old Google Maps had a label way off to the left to give me my explanation. It is now a battered women's shelter. That makes sense as the sanatorium was designed to be sequestered from society. It also rules it out as huntable grounds for men as most shelters have strict rules.

Credit : Google Maps

So I'll pass this up as a target and pass it on to the local metal detecting club to see if the women there can pitch a metal-detecting outreach day to the shelter.

Given that, I'll freeze any more research on it, and I'll write it off as another lukewarm research success.

Estimated research time spent: 20 minutes

Example 3 – Drive-in Theaters

Because I already have a 1954 topographic map in front of me, I look for other coin areas. One that catches my eye is drive-in theaters.

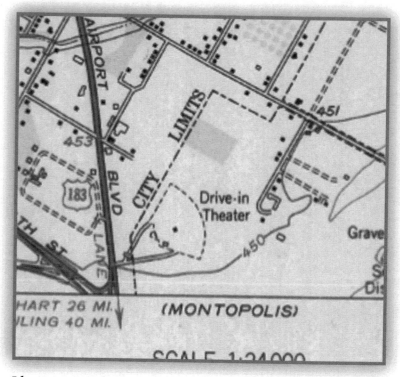

I begin to ponder how rich these targets are. Are people walking around much or mainly staying in their cars?

In their cars.

Are there lots of coins flowing, or just around concessions?

Just concessions.

Is the ground going to quickly hide dropped coins (like sawdust or gravel would), or is it paved?

Paved or hard-packed: if you drop a coin, you will likely hear it and pick it up easily, so there will not be a high rate of coin loss, although there will be coin loss.

I conclude that this is likely a Tier 3 coin zone, and while it will have some silver coins, there are far better targets on which to spend research time. Some coinshooters would argue against this point, given how many coins they can pull out of an old drive-in. My time, however, is more valuable, and I'll pass on Tier 3 targets.

A quick glance at Google shows two drive-in locations are now concrete jungles with office buildings.

I flat out kill this prospect and move on. No further time need be expended.

Estimated research time spent: 20 minutes

Example 4 – Random Coinshooting Lead

So before writing this book, I was researching for rare treasure books to add to my collection. I enjoy old treasure-tale books and prefer the ones from the turn of the century. However, they can be a bit hard to find, so I have to collect them in two steps:

a. Find out about them, and

b. Find a book dealer from whom to buy them.

The first is much harder than the second. I've found that old treasure magazines and bibliographies of treasure books are a good place to find advertisements and reviews on treasure books. In this case, I discovered some old treasure magazines that were scanned and put up on Scridb via TreasurereSearch. net, who appears to be known for a huge treasure magazine collection.

HOW TO RESEARCH FOR TREASURE HUNTING

I will be blunt and say that I have little faith in treasure magazines for leads. They are designed to sell magazines, not to generate good vetted leads. If you have ever read some of their articles, you will see how iffy their stories are. Many are rewrites of secondary sources which were, in turn, rewrites of secondary sources. So the end result is no better than a mud pie being sold as sirloin steak.

Magazines take stories from authors without fact checking or vetting of any kind, so long as the story plays well to the armchair treasure hunter audience. Because of these facts, I don't ever recommend treasure magazines as a source.

But back to my story. Near the ad for Foul Anchor books, I saw an article on a Texas ghost town near Denton called Gourlay, Texas. I will sum it up and say that the author claims that Spanish treasure was found nearby in a cave and that the Spanish were mining. This is the usual bullshit I see in THing magazines. This particular magazine was worse than average. However, for teaching purposes, it will make for a good example that will illustrate the value of good research.

GOURLAY, TEXAS
A GHOST TOWN
WITH A TREASURE

H. L. ALLEY

IN THE HISTORY OF THE OLD WEST, NAMES LIKE DODGE CITY, KANSAS, TOMBSTONE, ARIZONA, AND VIRGINIA CITY, NEVADA, WERE LINKED WITH VIOLENCE, GOLD AND DEATH. THESE TOWNS GREW UP IN A SAVAGE LAND WITH HARD TIMES AND IT TOOK MEN TWICE AS HARD AND SAVAGE TO TAME THEM. THE ROPE AND THE GUN WERE THE ONLY LAWS THEN, AND MORE OFTEN THAN NOT, IT WAS A CASE OF WHO SHOT OR HUNG WHOM FIRST. THE TOWN'S GUN THROWING, BLOODY DAYS ARE GONE FOREVER, BUT THEIR SHORT, VIOLENT HISTORIES ARE ENGRAVED ON THE TOMBSTONES IN EACH OF THEIR OVER-POPULATED BOOT HILL. THERE, IN JUST A FEW SHORT WORDS ON EACH TOMBSTONE, IS THE WRITTEN TESTIMONY OF THEIR VIOLENT AND BLOODY PAST.

Gourlay's only monument

THERE WAS ANOTHER TOWN IN THIS BLOODY ERA WHOSE NAME WAS NEVER AS FAMOUS AS TOMBSTONE, BUT WHOSE HISTORY WAS JUST AS VIOLENT. THAT TOWN WAS GOURLAY, TEXAS. A SMALL TOWN, IT STOOD A FEW MILES EAST OF DECATUR, TEXAS AND A SHORT DISTANCE SOUTH OF HIGHWAY 24. ALL THAT REMAINS OF GOURLAY TODAY, IS ONE OLD BUILDING WHOSE INHABITANTS HAVE LONG BEEN DEAD, AND WHOSE NAMES HAVE BEEN FORGOTTEN. IT WAS ONCE A THRIVING TOWN, BUT NOW INHABITED ONLY BY SNAKES AND LIZARDS, AND PERHAPS, ALTHOUGH ONE DOES NOT MENTION IT, A FEW OLD GHOSTS OF SOME OF THE PEOPLE WHO CAME TO A SUDDEN AND VIOLENT END.

Cave in background yeilded
Spanish coins and guns

THE GRAVEYARD, ABOUT AN ACRE SQUARE, IS OVERGROWN WITH UNDERBRUSH AND TREES. IT IS LOCATED AT THE NORTH END OF TOWN, A FEW YARDS FROM WHERE THE BLACKSMITH SHOP ONCE STOOD. THIS IS WHERE THE HISTORY OF GOURLAY IS RECORDED. SOME OF THE GRAVES HAVE FINE MARBLE TOMBSTONES, WHILE OTHERS ARE SANDSTONE WITH ONLY NAMES PRINTED IN A SIMPLE SCRAWL. ONE GRAVE, IS COVERED WITH ROCKS AND HAS ONE LARGE ROCK AS THE HEADSTONE. NO NAME IS RECORDED ON THE STONE, BUT IT IS THE GRAVE OF A CHRISTIAN INDIAN WHOSE NAME AND CAUSE OF DEATH ARE BOTH LOST TO HISTORY.

A RUSTY FENCE SURROUNDS THE GRAVE OF ONE OF THE SEVEN WIVES OF

Continued on page 22

Continued from page 15

ANDERSON LEWIS. HE WAS THE BLACK-SMITH OF GOURLAY, WHO MARRIED AND BURIED SIX WIVES. THE LAST ONE OUT-LIVED HIM, AND ALL SEVEN, PLUS MR. LEWIS, ARE BURIED IN THE SAME PLOT. ONE OF HIS SIX WIVES MUST HAVE BEEN FAVORITE, WHY ELSE IS ONLY ONE GRAVE SURROUNDED BY AN IRON FENCE?

IN STILL ANOTHER PLOT IN THE OLD GRAVEYARD, ARE THE GRAVES OF A MR. AND MRS. RAMSEY SALING, WHO DIED LESS THAN A DAY APART. THEY WERE AMONG THE FIRST SETTLERS IN THE TOWN, AND THEIR DOUBLE DEATHS CAUSED QUITE A STIR IN GOURLAY.

ANOTHER STIR WAS CAUSED WHEN THE MARLETT SISTERS ALSO DIED WITH-IN A DAY OF ONE ANOTHER. A DOUBLE FUNERAL WAS HELD AND THEY WERE LAID TO REST IN THE SAME PLOT.

GOURLAY ALSO HAD ITS VIOLENT DEATHS. ONE SUCH DEATH WAS THAT OF SIM OWENS, WHO WAS HUNG A SHORT DISTANCE FROM THE GRAVEYARD FOR CATTLE RUSTLING. HE WAS A MAN WHO HELPED HIS NEIGHBORS BY ROUNDING UP THEIR LOST STOCK FOR A SMALL FEE. BUT SOMEONE BECAME SUSPICIOUS, AND SAID THAT OWENS HIMSELF STOLE THE CATTLE, THEN "FOUND" THEM. THE SUS-PICION GREW, AND SOON SIM OWENS WAS CAUGHT AND HUNG AS A RUSTLER. THERE IS STILL A DISPUTE OVER WHETHER OR NOT HE WAS GUILTY. HE NOW LIES BURIED IN THE GRAVEYARD OF GOURLAY, WITH THE SIMPLE LETTERS, "SIM OWENS" PRINTED ON A SLAB OF SANDSTONE.

A NEWCOMER TO THE TOWN, WHOSE NAME HAS LONG BEEN FORGOTTEN, WAS SHOT FROM AMBUSH ONE DAY. HE CAME TO THE TOWN IN A SHINY NEW RIG, PULLED BY TWO BEAUTIFULLY MATCHED HORSES. HE BOUGHT SOME LAND, AND BUILT A HOUSE. ONE DAY WHILE DOING HIS CHORES, HE WAS SHOT. HIS HORSES AND RIG WERE STOLEN AND THERE IS NO RECORD OF HIS MURDERER EVER BEING APPREHENDED.

THEN ONE NIGHT A NEGRO MAN WAS SHOT BY MISTAKE WHILE CHECKING ON HIS MASTER'S LIVESTOCK. FOR MONTHS, CATTLE HAD BEEN STOLEN FROM A COM-POUND, AND A GROUP OF MEN ORGANIZED TO TRY AND CATCH THE THIEF OR THE THEIVES. THEY WAITED AT THE CORRAL WITH RIFLES, AND WHEN THE UNSUS-PECTING NEGRO MAN SHOWED UP, HE WAS SHOT BY ONE MAN IN THE GROUP. IT WAS AN UNFORTUNATE ACCIDENT.

ON THE BANKS OF THE WINDING CREEK WHERE GOURLAY WAS BUILT, IS AN OLD INDIAN BURIAL GROUND THAT HAS NEVER BEEN LOCATED. A FEW ARTI-FACTS THAT WERE FOUND THERE HAVE BEEN CARRIED OFF BY VISITORS TO GOURLAY, WITH THE EXCEPTION OF A HUGE SLAB ROCK WHERE THE INDIANS

Artifacts and coins found
in Gourlay by author.

GROUND THEIR GRAIN. A MYRIOS OF FOSSILS CAN BE FOUND ALONG THE CREEK. THESE ARE EVIDENCE THAT THE AREA WAS ONCE COVERED BY WATER.

SOUTHEAST OF GOURLAY, IS A CAVE IN WHICH HAS BEEN FOUND SOME OLD SPANISH WEAPONS, THREE GOLD DOUB-LOONS AND SEVERAL PIECES-OF-EIGHT. IN THE PAST THE CAVE WAS LARGE E-NOUGH TO RIDE A HORSE INTO, BUT IN THE RECENT YEARS IT HAS CAVED IN.

SOME SPANIARDS SETTLED IN THIS SECTION OF WISE COUNTY, TEXAS IN THE MIDDLE SEVENTEEN HUNDREDS, AND FOUND SILVER AT A LOCATION NEARBY. A MINE SHAFT WAS SUNK AND SEVERAL TONS OF SILVER WAS MINED. EVEN-TUALLY, THEY WERE ATTACKED BY IN-DIANS, A BATTLE FOLLOWED, THEN THE INDIANS WITHDREW TO POW-WOW AND MAKE READY FOR ANOTHER ATTACK. IT WAS DURING THE LULL AFTER THE FIRST ATTACK THAT THE SPANISH DECIDED TO BURY WHAT SILVER THEY HAD ALREADY

Continued on page 28

Ghost Towns Continued from page 22

TAKEN OUT OF THE MINE. AFTER IT WAS BURIED, A MAP WAS MADE OF THE LOCATION. THE INDIANS ATTACKED A-GAIN AND ALL OF THE SPANIARDS WERE KILLED. THE KNOWLEDGE OF THE WHERE-ABOUTS OF THE SILVER DIED WITH THEM.

A FEW YEARS BACK, I WAS TOLD BY A MAN THAT HE HAD FOUND A MAP WITH SOME SPANISH SIGNS ON IT IN A LEATH-ER POUCH IN THE HOLLOW OF A TREE. HE SAID THIS MAP GAVE THE EXACT LO-CATION TO A HIDDEN SPANISH SILVER TREASURE. AFTER STUDYING THE MAP, I FOUND OUT THAT IT WAS THE MAP OF THE BURIED SILVER TREASURE NEAR GOURLAY. THE MAN TOLD ME THAT HE HAD SINCE LOST THE MAP, BUT HE HAD MEMORIZED IT. HE SAID THAT THE TREASURE WAS BURIED BETWEEN TWO LARGE OAK TREES, WITH SIGNS CARVED ON EACH. I THANKED HIM FOR THIS IN-FORMATION, AND THOUGHT TO MYSELF, THAT SOMEDAY I WOULD GO TO GOURLAY AND TRY TO FIND THIS TREASURE.

THAT SOMEDAY FINALLY CAME. A FRIEND AND I SET OUT TO SEE IF WE REALLY COULD FIND THE BURIED TREA-SURE. WHEN WE GOT TO THE LOCATION, WE HAD NO TROUBLE FINDING THE TWO LARGE TREES AS WE HAD SOME SPECIFIC DIRECTIONS TO FOLLOW. WE STARTED OUR DIGGING RIGHT AWAY, AND HAD ONLY DUG ABOUT TWO FEET WHEN WE HIT A LAYER OF LOGS THAT WERE LAID CRISS-CROSS. WE REMOVED THESE, AND DUG DOWN ABOUT THREE MORE FEET AND HIT SOME MORE LOGS THAT WERE LAID IN THE SAME FASHION AS THE FIRST ONES. WE THEN REMOVED THOSE LOGS, AND DUG SOME MORE, SUDDENLY, TROUBLE DEVEL-OPED, IT WAS SEEP SAND. FOR EVERY SHOVEL-FULL OF SAND REMOVED, THAT MUCH WOULD SEEP RIGHT BACK IN AGAIN.

WE KNEW WE COULD NOT SHOVEL THE SAND OUT, SO A DECISION WAS MADE TO BUILD A SHAFT OF LUMBER ALONG THE SIDES OF THE HOLE AS WE DUG. WHEN WE HAD GONE DOWN ABOUT TEN FEET IN-TO THE SAND, WE KNEW IT WAS NO USE, FOR THE SILVER TREASURE KEPT SINK-ING INTO THE SOFT DEEP SAND, UNTIL IT WAS OUT OF THE RANGE OF THE DE-TECTOR. WE DID NOT HAVE THE TIME TO KEEP ON DIGGING TO SEE IF WE COULD DIG BELOW THE SEEP SAND, SO THE HUNT WAS ABANDONED. OUR PLANS NOW ARE TO DRILL A 12-INCH HOLE IN-TO THE TREASURE SITE TO SEE WHAT WE CAN FIND. WE HOPE THIS ATTEMPT WILL BE SUCCESSFUL. IN THE MEANTIME, IS ANYONE INTERESTED IN A BURIED SPAN-ISH TREASURE?

LOST MINES

Credit: the Archivist, January 1967, Shown under Fair Use.

So my lead, which may be valuable, is a Texas ghost town which may be good for coinshooting. (Hopefully, it is not a ghost town, but a ghost hamlet that didn't make it into the Texas ghost town books. I'd really like to find a virgin spot.)

For the whole Spanish mine and treasure thing, I write all that off as BS. This region of Texas has no igneous rock, and no precious metal mining ever occurred here. I have a Bureau of Economic Geology-issued booklet on mining in Texas to back me up on that.[15]

---

15. Gold and Silver in Texas by Thomas J Evans, Mineral Resource Circular No. 56, Bureau of Economic Geology.

Further, the author's bias was to sell an article to a treasure magazine, so I've completely discounted that portion of his story. But I want to check about the potential ghost town.

The thing I did was a basic Shallow Web check on Google for "Gourlay Texas." Nada.

Hmm. Interesting.

I know the state of Texas has a good online index of state history stuff, called Texas State Historical Association's "Handbook of Texas Online." So I pop in Gourlay again and get zilch.

Hmm. BS story?

Well, the initial story mentions a graveyard. So I go back and Google "Gourlay cemetery." I get some hits, and one mentions a genealogist finding the Gourlay, aka Lewis Cemetery, in 2002.

Hey, that is good news.

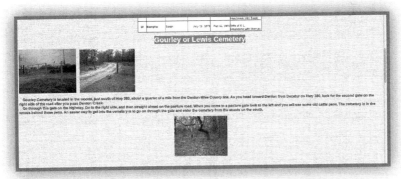

She even outlines how she drove there and publishes some low-res pictures. Her description of the location closely matches the original lead story.

Even better.

The information in the table below came from headstone pictures taken in March of 2002.
Information in parenthesis ( ) came from the cemetery listings done in January 1967 by Mr. & Mrs. Homer L. Roper and Mr. & Mrs. Cletus Johnston. They were able to
headstones that I did not find [# is in brackets]. I found 6 headstones that they did not find.
The information about Anderson Lewis was sent in by Chinka Pace.

#	Last Name	First Name	Born	Date of Death	Information Notes
14	Papito	James			
29	Bur? (Burrow)	Codetta	no date		
[28]	Cates	Bobbie	Jan 19, 1880	June 9, 1894	Son of J.G. & M.E.
18	Chisholm	Susan Linch	Feb 21, 1859 (1863)	Jan 21, 1889 (1882)	Daughter of G.W. & C.O. (S.C.) Linch - Wife of W.N.
1	Gipson or Gibson	Jessy H.	Oct 8, 1840	Feb 8, 1886	Name is Gipson on headstone and Gibson on footstone
36	Goforth	G.W.	Oct 18, ?(1860)	Feb 1, 1880	
17	Grimes	J.L.	Apr 29, 1915	Apr 29, 1915	Infant son of M. & Mrs. J.H.
20	Huley	Willie	(1854)	(Feb 24, 1925)	
[32]	Knox	?			
10	Lewis	Arthen (Woodson O.)	(Aug 11, 1868)	Aug 1888	
4	Lewis	Anderson	July 18, 1826	Feb 16, 1887	Came from Ohio - Married 5 times after 1st wife Nancy Manda - Married to Alpha Ross in 1880)
11	Lewis	David			

What is really interesting is that she puts down all the names on the headstones in a chart. From that chart, I can tell the population size of Gourlay, which isn't much. I'm assuming more aren't buried in other unmarked graveyards nearby. Thus, this ghost town is looking more like a hamlet. The names are very similar, and it begins to look like a family compound with multiple generations living nearby. The website about the cemetery called it "Gourlay" or "Lewis," which now makes sense as most are from the Lewis family. As an encouragement, the genealogist states:

> "We think that 'Gourley' may have been a settlement with at least a store and school at one time."

Hmmm, she spells it differently. Better check both spellings. I back up and recheck Texas History Online again, nada. Good, I think.

From her account, we know our target—detect the school and the store, and if possible, the house of the store owner.

I head to Archive.org to see what old county history books are available for Wise County, Texas. I discover a single book for Wise, called Pioneer History of Wise County by Cates, 1907. That should be a good, relevant book.

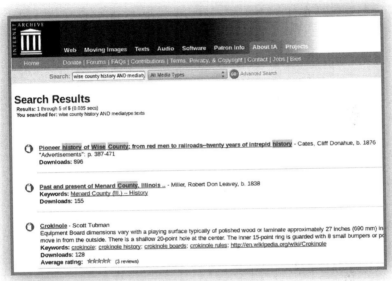

I'd like to find Gourley in the book. But after using the "full text" option and a search for both Gourlay and Gourley, I come up empty. There are several mentions of Lewis, however.

A BookFinder.com search finds another county book I should check out, *Centennial History of Wise County 1853-1953* by Mary Cates and Moore, which I'd have to find at a library. I do take note of the name, Cates, and recognize that research done by her relative will have a bias.

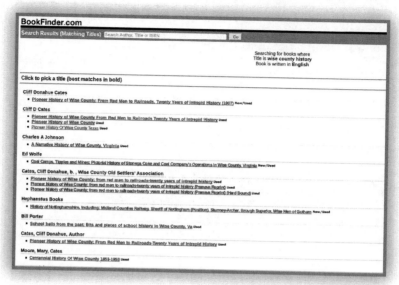

Next I head to Worldcat.org to find which nearby libraries have it. As a scarce book, the closest library turns out to be the state archive library.

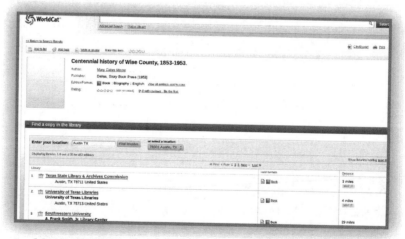

I add the book to my wish list of books to review at the state archives for my next visit.

So, I've vetted the story some, and the author very likely visited the area in the '60s. He mentioned a building standing, and I want to find that building on a USGS overflight image or a USGS topographic map.

A search of USGS finds a Decatur map from the '60s. However, I don't see any reference to a graveyard or a building south of 380. I do confirm that 380 is the old Highway 24 mentioned in the original lead story. Therefore, I'm upgrading the authority of parts of the story.

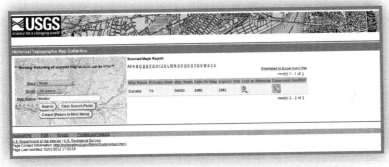

First item is to locate what map assets are available.
This is often harder than you think.

Credit: USGS

The edge of the topo says "Bluett" where the next map is. So I get back to USGS topos and find the next part of the map. Bluett 1960.

Here, I don't see any dot where I think the building should be according to the vague descriptions from the genealogist. But he described a building standing, and the genealogist described old cattle pens, so these features should show up in an aerial overflight. So, next I need to find what overflights will be available from the USGS.

Over at EarthExplorer.usgs.gov, I define a red square that represents the area where I think the graveyard and, hence, the building are located. I see there are several images: one from the '50s and several from the '60s. By checking the footprint and metadata, I see the '50s overflight was high at 30,000 feet, and the resolution is low. There is a May 1, 1968, overflight at a much lower 12,000 feet, with much better resolution, and it has been scanned at high resolution.

North is not always up on USGS aerial images, be careful. Credit:USGS.

I download the image and have to rotate it to get north up. Next is the time-consuming task of lining up the image with the current Google Maps image to figure out where the image covers.

As a note, the high-res scanned historical images can be 10-90 MB in size, so you need a program that can handle big images and can rotate them. This particular photo was 78 MB.

After an hour of rereading the genealogist's account, the original story, and looking at Google's imagery (which isn't as good as the 1968 overflight), I finally think I've spotted the derelict building pointed out in the article. It had an asymmetric roof, and if you look carefully at the aerial photograph, you'll spot the asymmetric shadow. I can't spot the graveyard, but when I ask permission from the landowners, I'll ask where it is. I do have enough information to make a field reconnaissance and maybe hunt.

I also note that southwest of the building there are several soil marks. These may or may not be old buildings. However, I'd be quick to detect those locations.

Wanting a better view of the old building, I use EarthExplorer again to grab an HRO (High Resolution Orthorectified) Image. USGS had an archived image from 2007. In this image, the building is clearly collapsed.

I'd also put a visit to the Wise county historical society on my list because it seems to have a splendid old building and a good archive. The idea for a visit would be to see if I can garner more information on Gourlay with the intent of finding a map that may outline the school and the store.

Next, I will need to go into the field to establish ground truth by locating the graveyard and the collapsed building. I would get a GPS fix on the building for future reference.

Estimated time in research: 4 hours, with two more research trips off site left to do.

CHAPTER NINETEEN

ADDRESS THE COST OF RESEARCH VERSUS EXPLORING

Doing good research isn't free. The most expensive part of it will be your time. Or more specifically, your opportunity cost, which represents the income you could have made with your time. Use your time wisely. (The mantra again.)

On top of time, there may be travel costs such as gas and wear and tear on vehicles going to and from libraries, the cost of inter-library loan fees for rare books, travel and lodging costs for trips to the state archives, or even flight costs for trips to faraway cities or national archives.

On the flip side, starting a project and spending time in a field swinging a detector without proper research is horribly expensive. You can waste an enormous amount of time, which makes for a huge opportunity cost. Imagine all the goodies you could have found if you had done your research first!

In conclusion, research is the best way to minimize your cost of treasure hunting and detecting.

CHAPTER TWENTY

WIZARD'S FIRST RULE AND THE KGC

I wanted to title this chapter, "Why the KGC (Knights of the Golden Circle) just won't die and how to kill it and legends like it," but I think Goodkind captured this best with Wizard's First Rule.

Terry Goodkind, author of Wizard's First Rule[16], came up with a nice name for a common mental trap. He called it Wizard's First Rule. The name succinctly captures the essence of a common judgment flaw to which we can easily fall prey.

The rule is this:

> "Because people are stupid, they will believe a lie because they want to believe it's true, or because they are afraid it might be true." –T. Goodkind

With treasure hunting, we very much want our suspicions to be true. Be aware of this when researching, keep your feet

---

16. Wizard's First Rule: Sword of Truth, 1994, Terry Goodkind.

solidly on the ground, and don't start believing your theories are true unless evidence corroborates you. Keep your perspective in check.

Wizard's First Rule is why the KGC treasure myths are alive and kicking. Even I want to believe in secret societies, Confederate gold, mysterious hoards in secret bunkers, and elaborate triangulation methods that require surveyors to find them. Unfortunately, it is just bullshit fiction.

Yes, there was a KGC. Good research can easily prove it. There were KGC documents,[17] ephemera, primary source books,[18] sister castle groups advertisements (so much for secret!), and court cases to prove it. Some members did try to fight the Union subversively; there were even paramilitary actions. However, eventually they were just a fifth columnist group that simply petered out. The historical record even shows that they were underfunded, which is ironic given the billions folks claim they buried.

The idea that they had a massive gold hoard given to them by a broke government to be buried for the South to rise again and to be protected by dirt poor country hillbillies . . . that is . . . well . . . ummm . . . entertaining?

At best, Confederates paymaster officers with payrolls buried their payroll to avoid Union forces obtaining it. The vast majority were dug up later by these officers or corrupt companions for personal use. A small percentage of them are still buried, but these will likely be only a few hundred dollars in face value.

---

17. An Authentic Exposition of the KGC, Knights of the Golden Circle, 1861.
18. Treason History of the Order of Sons of Liberty, by Felix Stidger, 1864.

CHAPTER TWENTY-ONE

GUTS

GUTS stands for Go Use This Stuff!

Knowing how to do something is worthless if you don't go use it! You have made it to the end.

It depresses me when I remember the statistic from a study the Jenkens Group put out about the number of people who don't finish a book—57 percent—so the number who act on it will be even smaller. But if you are reading this, you've made it.

By all means, you now have the unfair advantage of excellent research knowledge. Go forth, use it, and find your treasure!

Good luck, good hunting!

CHAPTER TWENTY-TWO

CHECKLIST FOR RESEARCH

☐ County History Book

☐ Regional History Book

☐ Archive.org Supporting History Books

☐ Other Supporting History Books (from Library or Collection)

☐ WPA Book for the Area

☐ USGS Topo Maps

☐ USGS Historic Imagery

☐ Sanborn (if available)

☐ County Plats (Optional)

Made in the USA
Middletown, DE
16 March 2016